Is Your Data Secure?

Gobinath Radhakrishnan
Asif Hussain
Nirmal Kumar Veeraraghavan
Pushparaj Vijayan

DOYENSYS
Technology Drives, We Lead

notionpress
.com

INDIA · SINGAPORE · MALAYSIA

Notion Press

Old No. 38, New No. 6
McNichols Road, Chetpet
Chennai - 600 031

First Published by Notion Press 2019
Copyright © Doyensys 2019
All Rights Reserved.

ISBN 978-1-64760-815-6

CONTENTS

CONTENTS

CONTENTS

CONTENTS

ON-PREMISE DATA SECURITY

DATA PROTECTION

Data is a new currency in the modern world of functioning. Nowadays, we even face the issue of data theft, which is very sensitive. Just imagine what happens if the public sector loses their sensitive data against the attack. The threat over data changes considerably nowadays, and therefore, securing data is more crucial.

Adding to this are on-going payment product occasions where clients download malware that scrambles their information and adequately denies them access to it until they make an instalment to a mysterious aggressor. The requirement for improved answers to ensure information has never been more prominent.

Notwithstanding the fiscal and reputational misfortunes emerging from information ruptures, associations today work in an inexorably stringent and quick-developing administrative scene. Many companies are migrating their workloads to the cloud and embracing new, agile deployment models such as containers and micro-services. Although cloud deployments can provide a higher degree of application security, they also change trust boundaries and can expose data to new threats (we will look into this in detail in Chapter 2). As a result, data security controls need to scale and work seamlessly across on-premises, private cloud, public cloud, and hybrid cloud environments.

A well-structured data security solution must provide controls to mitigate these various threat vectors and more. The best approach is a built-in framework of security controls, which can be deployed easily and which enables organizations to apply appropriate levels of security controls to the data being managed. The main components of securing database deployments are shown in the graphic below and include the following types of controls:

- ☐ *Evaluative controls* include tools for evaluating the security posture of a database, including the ability to monitor and identify configuration changes.
- ☐ *Preventive controls* block unauthorised access to data by leveraging technologies such as encryption, masking and subsetting and by restricting access to application data by unauthorised users.
- ☐ *Detective controls* monitor user and application data access behaviour, allowing administrators to detect and block threats and support compliance reporting.
- ☐ *Data-driven security* enforces user- and application-level data access controls at the source, within the database, providing consistent, strong security for application data.

Types of Database Security Controls

This chapter illustrates how to secure data in on-premises and covers different aspects of database security in on-premises.

1. Authentication and Authorization
2. Enforcing Separation of Duty
3. Data-Driven Application Authorization
4. Protecting Data using Oracle Maximum Availability Architecture
5. General Guidance for a Better Infrastructure

Finally, in the Conclusion, we bring all of the technologies together to show how to make better standards to improvise the security of an organization's data according to the organization requirements. This book walks through in-depth all of the above concepts.

AUTHENTICATION AND AUTHORIZATION

In any format of data, it should be good that it has proper authentication and authorization. The first step in securing a database is validating the identity of the user (authentication) and what action they can perform against the data. Frequent attacks to steal sensitive team from the database include the following ways:

- ☐ Search for a default/published password.
- ☐ A weak DB password with no limits on password retries.
- ☐ Find hardcoded DB connection information.
- ☐ Social engineering to over-privileged accounts.

Types of Database Users

It is essential to provide sufficient authorization to perform tasks without providing unnecessary additional privileges. Some user tasks include

1. Database Administrator (DBA)
   a. Database Startup and Shutdown
   b. Database Patching
   c. Database Performance Tuning
   d. Database Upgrade
   e. Database backup and Recovery
2. Application User
   a. Application Maintain account
   b. Application Users Accounts

3. Security Administrator User

    a. User Account Management
    b. Audit Management
    c. Encryption Key Management

Database Administrator (DBA) accounts ordinarily have wide access to the database to do their undertakings. Their exceptionally favoured database likewise gives them access to delicate database information (individual, wellbeing and corporate fund records) that are not required to perform DBA assignments. DBAs ought not to utilise shared records like SYSTEM; however, they use named accounts with solid confirmation to give responsibility on database occasions. DBA records ought to likewise have custom-fitted benefits for individual undertakings and obligations to decrease the assault surface related to these records. As a component of typical investigation or to achieve another undertaking, DBAs ought to be conceded additional benefits and jobs, which can be disavowed a short time later if not required any longer. So it creates a named user for each database team member.

Application DBA and application administration accounts in the database additionally gather benefits and jobs. Much of the time, the application administration accounts in the database incorporate not just every one of the jobs and benefits required for the benefit of each client to get to application information, yet in addition jobs and benefits to perform application overhauls, patches, and other upkeep exercises. These extra jobs and benefits are not exclusively required for runtime application execution, they are as often as possible not evacuated after upkeep. Application DBAs who work with the application pattern should just approach the application blueprint objects, yet they are sometimes given database-wide benefits because it is simpler than conceding individual article benefits.

Security Administrator needs one of a kind access to oversee security controls, encryption keys, database clients, and review records. Partition of obligation needs to exist between database heads/clients and security executives to counteract DBA/client accounts from having the option to modify security records, make counterfeit clients, and change security controls. Security overseers should be constrained to their errands, so they do not have wide access to the delicate information in the database, notwithstanding dealing with the security controls.

Overseeing database assets for DBA, application, and client records is additionally essential to guarantee records that cannot coincidentally or malignantly affect utilization of the database by another record. Client limitations on tablespaces, inactive time, and the number of simultaneous sessions are fundamental asset contemplations to counteract sway on different clients.

Users and Schema

In the Oracle Database, clients, patterns, and records are, for the most part, thought to be proportional. A record contains mapping articles like tables, lists, and methodology. Nevertheless, as the database is advancing to work with composition-less application clients and with patterns, a more grounded separation should be made between these terms.

Client records are of two sorts: application clients and database clients. Application clients might not have any database account affiliation (composition-less clients). A database client record has related outlines and items. A database pattern can be mapped to an application client (selective mapping) or to different application clients (shared mapping).

Schema-only accounts introduced in Oracle Database 18c are accounts with a named pattern, however, with no capacity to login. Various Oracle records give diagram articles to applications; however, they do not require applications or clients to login to the composition account. Earlier, these records would have passwords that would be occasionally turned. With mapping just accounts, there are no passwords, so vindictive clients cannot endeavour to login to these records. Different clients can, at present, be allowed with perused/composed access to these patterns.

Authentication Methods

Prophet underpins various methods for verification, including passwords put away locally inside the database or in unified catalogue administrations. Clients can likewise be confirmed by the working framework, Utilizing the IDENTIFIED EXTERNALLY condition when making the client, or by different outer validation administrations, including Kerberos, open key endorsements, and RADIUS.

Passwords are utilised for single-direction verification of the client to the database, whereas Kerberos and public key certification support confirmation guaranteeing the client are to be sure associating with the best possible database. The accompanying table records the database verification techniques and related mappings to patterns and jobs.

Authentication method	Schema is mapping	Role mapping
Password authentication	Schema is the same as the user	Managed in database
OS authentication	Schema is mapped to the user	Managed in the database and also able to map OS groups to roles
Kerberos authentication	Schema is mapped to the user	Managed in database
Public key certificate authentication	Schema is mapped to the user	Managed in database
RADIUS authentication	Schema is mapped to the user	Managed in database, optionally through a RADIUS server
LDAP (Lightweight Directory Access Protocol) directory authentication	Managed in database or directory service	Managed in database and directory service

Application Services Authentication

With password validation, clients are relied upon to give a secret key when they interface with the database; however, applications, middle-tier framework, and batch jobs cannot rely upon a human to type the password. Previously, a typical method to give passwords was to insert client names and passwords in the code or in contents.

This expanded the assault surface against the database, and individuals needed to ensure that their contents were not uncovered. Additionally, if passwords were ever changed, changes to the contents were required. One arrangement is to store password accreditations in a customer side Oracle wallet. An Oracle wallet is utilised to store password and authentication, including passwords, private keys, and certificates.

The utilization of wallets lessens dangers on the grounds that the passwords are never again uncovered on order line history, and secret key administration strategies are all the more effectively authorised without changing application code at whatever point client names or passwords change. To design the utilization of password put away on an Oracle wallet, set the WALLET_LOCATION parameter in the customer's sqlnet.ora document. Applications would then be able to associate with the database without giving login accreditations.

Authentication Using Proxy

Application administrators frequently need to access an application schema for support. Different application users having a similar application schema username and password to interface with the schema give no responsibility and make it hard to review and explore issues.

Oracle introduced proxy users so that administrators could connect to application schemas for maintenance activities without having to share passwords and provide an audit of the actual database user who performed the actions. Proxy authentication allows the administrators to authenticate with their own credentials first and then proxy to the application schema. In such cases, the audit records show the actual user who performed the maintenance activities.

This form of proxy authentication is supported in Oracle Call Interface (OCI), (Java Database Connectivity) JDBC, and on the SQL*PLUS command line. Here is an example where the user alice_appdba is allowed to connect to the database and act as hrapp (application schema).

SQL> ALTER USER hrapp GRANT CONNECT THROUGH alice_appdba;

Now the user alice_appdba can connect using her own password and assume the identity and privileges of the hrapp schema by proxy as follows:

SQL> CONNECT alice_appdba[hrapp]

Enter password: <alice_appdba_password>

The proxy user is the one that is logged in the audit and is not the hrapp account.

Database Authentication

Authorization grants permission to perform a specific operation, such as accessing a particular object. Authorizations are granted to subjects, which may include individual users, roles, or programs acting on behalf of users. In Oracle, authorization is done through the privilege and role mechanism.

A database privilege grants the ability to access data objects or execute statements. There are three types of privileges—object, system and administrative. Object privileges are fine-grained privileges to perform actions on specific data objects or execute specific procedures. These are the typical privileges given to applications and users in the database. Examples include privileges to read data from a table (SELECT or READ), execute a PL/SQL statement (EXECUTE), and alter table structure (ALTER). System privileges are typically used by database administrators for application or database maintenance.

System privileges like SELECT ANY TABLE allow the user to read data from almost any table in the database, including sensitive data stored in application schemas. CREATE USER is another example of a system privilege allowing accounts to be created for new users in the database.

Administrative privileges are used for specific tasks like database backup, encryption key management, and database operations (e.g., startup and shutdown). Certain maintenance activities like database upgrade and patching must be done by the SYS account (database owner).

The administrative privilege SYSDBA is used to allow a user to become SYS for these tasks.

The SYS account and the related SYSDBA administrative privilege should only be used when necessary and be safeguarded using a privileged access management system.

Roles

Roles are groups of privileges that make it easier to manage privileges for users. Multiple users can be granted the same role to simplify privilege management for users. Direct object and system privileges can be grouped into task-based roles. Different clients can be allowed to do a similar job to improve benefiting the executives for clients. Roles can likewise be progressively assembled under different roles. This enables privileges to be gathered in a task job, and numerous task roles can be assembled for a hierarchical job.

Data Dictionary

One of the most important parts of an Oracle Database is its **data dictionary**, which is a **read-only** set of tables that provides information about the database. A data dictionary contains:

- the definitions of all schema objects in the database (tables, views, indexes, clusters, synonyms, sequences, procedures, functions, packages, triggers, and so on);
- how much space has been allocated for, and is currently used by, the schema objects;
- default values for columns;
- integrity constraint information;
- the names of Oracle users;
- privileges and roles each user has been granted;
- auditing information, such as who has accessed or updated various schema objects and
- other general database information

The data dictionary is structured in tables and views, just like other database data. All of the data dictionary tables and views for a given database are stored in that database's SYSTEM tablespace.

Not only is the data dictionary central to every Oracle Database, but also it is an important tool for all users, from end-users to application designers and database administrators. Use SQL statements to access the data dictionary. Because the data dictionary is read-only, you can issue only queries (SELECT statements) against its tables and views.

The dictionary views listed below show the roles and privileges granted to users or roles.

Dictionary Views	Contents	
DBA_TAB_PRIVS	Object privilege grants to roles or users	
DBA_SYS_PRIVS	System privilege grants to roles or users	
DBA_ROLE_PRIVS	Role grants to users or other roles	
DBA_ROLES	All defined roles	

If one were to analyse the information in these tables, he/she would see that the out-of-the-box Oracle DBA role is extremely powerful, with more than two hundred system privileges (depending on what database options were installed) including ALTER SESSION; CREATE, ALTER and DROP USER; CREATE and ALTER ANY TABLE; SELECT, INSERT, UPDATE, and DELETE ANY TABLE; EXPORT and IMPORT FULL DATABASE, and over eighty roles. The Oracle DBA role should not be modified or used by the customer. Each organization should create a custom DBA role (i.e., ops_dba, backup_dba) that has the roles and privileges required for that role.

User Profile

A profile is utilised to make a typical approach of password and resource authorization parameters for client accounts. User accounts are then related and authorised with a profile arrangement to disentangle the executives of regular policies over an organization. The policy below (org_profile) incorporates both password and asset authorization parameters. The asset authorization parameters in as far as possible an association time of an hour and a half permit just two sessions for every client account and naturally logout clients following 30 minutes of persistent inactive time.

Utilizing benefits and jobs in this design makes it simple to add another individual to an organization. They would be conceded the job for the situation as opposed to finding every one of the benefits required and giving them individually. As associations change and undertakings move, starting with one gathering and then onto the next, the assignment jobs can be basically moved as opposed to overseeing individual benefits or reclassifying all of the hierarchical level jobs. Jobs disentangle the administration of client benefits when there is a hierarchical change.

SUMMARY

Now we come to know how to protect data by using users and authorization is most important in data access. Without controlling any user, it highly risks always associated with the security of data. This can be controlled locally and centrally. In the upcoming chapter, we will be finding the right number of privileges and roles that can quickly be done using Oracle Database Vault's Privilege Analysis. Proper use of privileges and roles to limit user access, combined with strong authentication, sets the foundation for a secure database.

ENFORCING SEPARATION OF DUTY

This part presents best practices, for example, the least benefit model and partition of obligation for controlling access by privileged user accounts. It talks about how Oracle Database Vault keeps privileged users from Utilizing their framework benefits to get to delicate information and furthermore to anticipate accidental or malicious changes to the database. It proceeds with how Oracle Database Vault helps execute the least benefit model and separation of duty.

Separation of duty, as a security principle, has as its primary objective the prevention of fraud and errors. This objective is achieved by disseminating the tasks and associated privileges for a specific business process among multiple users. This principle is demonstrated in the traditional example of separation of duty found in the requirement of two signatures on a check. Previous work on separation of duty requirements often explored implementations based on role-based access control (RBAC) principles.

These implementations are concerned with constraining the associations between RBAC components, namely users, roles, and permissions. Enforcement of the separation of duty requirements, although being an integrity requirement, thus relies on an access control service that is sensitive to the separation of duty requirements. A distinction between the separation of duty requirements that can be enforced in administrative environments, namely static separation of duty, and requirements that can only be implemented in a runtime environment, namely dynamic separation of duty, is required.

It is argued that RBAC does not support the complex work processes often associated with the separation of duty requirements, particularly with dynamic separation of duty. The workflow environment, being primarily concerned with the facilitation of complex work processes, provides a context in which the specification of separation of duty requirements can be studied.

Privileged users have incredible powerful system privileges, which give them unrestricted access to the database so they can, without much of a stretch, deal with the database. Nevertheless, this gives the administrative accounts full access to all of the touchy information in the database, for example, pay, SSN, aadhar number, organization money-related estimates and protected innovation. Programmers typically use spear-phishing assaults to target privileged users in an association. While you most likely trust your DBAs, external programmers can use a similar DBA, and a privileged client represents malignant use. Cybersecurity has a concern for those users.

How to Control Those Users

Privileged users require powerful roles to support and maintain databases. Without that, they are not able to do their task in a faster manner. Organization concerns employees and their sensitive data from unauthorised users. Therefore, there should be a balance between these two requirements to smoothly run business without compromising the needs. For example, DBA users always have to select any table privilege, and then they will be able to view all of the details including intellectual property and other sensitive data; also with the help of the system, apps schema is able to modify data too in case of misinterpretation. There are many ways to limit this kind of issues and protect sensitive data.

Least Privileged: The name itself explains that those users execute least/minimum set of operations based on their job nature. In case if any attackers are found to be those users, the amount of threat is also limited against a database. It is better to create roles rather than the border access category.

Separation of Duty: Closely related to the principle of least privilege is the concept of separation of duty. This is the notion that administration tasks should be divided among several users instead of a single powerful individual with full access to all database administration, operations, and security controls. Dividing administrative, operations and security duties make it less likely for privileged users to abuse their privileges because any single administrator will only have a portion of the privileges.

Named Users: It is easy to see users share their password for convenience. However, it increases the risk and reduces accountability (even it is their responsibility) because this habit results in many people accessing the same account for their convenience. Say we have one local user in R12 account and all DBA users are using the same, then it is difficult to find who modified any record (even though it shows some user name in record history).

Sys Owner Account: SYSDBA is an administrative privilege that provides full access to the SYS (database owner) account. The use of this privilege and account should be limited to when it is required, such as during database upgrades and patching. Change management and privileged access management (PAM) systems should be used to control access to this privilege.

Audit Protections: Audit records provide an irrefutable record of actions taken whether they are generated by a database, directory, or an operating system. Informations such as privileged user actions that were taken (CREATE USER, CREATE ANY TABLE, ALTER SYSTEM, and ALTER SESSION) coupled with the context of the event such as the initiating IP address, event time, and actual SQL statement, are just a few examples of audit information needed in compliance and forensic reports.

These best practices are well-known, but are difficult to enforce without specific technologies. Oracle Database Vault enforces separation of duties, introduces realms to prevent access to sensitive data regardless of system privileges, and provides command rules to prevent accidental or malicious SQL commands. Oracle Database Vault also includes a powerful privilege analysis tool to determine a set of privileges and roles needed for a given set of operations. Oracle Database Vault makes it easier for administrators to follow and enforce good security practices for their database.

Least Privilege and Separation of Duty

To support the principles of least privilege and separation of duty, the SYSOPER administrative privilege allows an administrator to perform limited tasks such as starting and stopping the database without having the full range of powers conferred by the SYSDBA privilege. The main types of user privileges are as follows:

System privileges: A system privilege gives a user the ability to perform a particular action or to perform an action on any schema objects of a particular type. For example, the system privilege CREATE TABLE permits a user to create tables in the schema associated with that user, and the system privilege CREATE USER permits a user to create database users.

Object privileges: An object privilege gives a user the ability to perform a particular action on a specific schema object. Different object privileges are available for different types of schema objects. The privileges to select rows from the EMPLOYEES table or to delete rows from the DEPARTMENTS table are examples of object privileges.

Roles Name	Description
Connect	Enables a user to connect to the database. Grants this role to any user or application that needs database access.
Resource	Enables a user to create, modify, and delete certain types of schema objects in the schema associated with that user. Grants this role only to developers and to other users that must create schema objects. This role grants a subset of the create object system privileges. For example, it grants the CREATE TABLE system privilege, but does not grant the CREATE VIEW system privilege. It grants only the following privileges: CREATE CLUSTER, CREATE INDEXTYPE, CREATE OPERATOR, CREATE PROCEDURE, CREATE SEQUENCE, CREATE TABLE, CREATE TRIGGER, and CREATE TYPE.
DBA	Enables a user to perform most administrative functions, including creating users and granting privileges; creating and granting roles; creating, modifying, and deleting schema objects in any schema; and more. It grants all system privileges, but does not include the privileges to start or shut down the database instance. It is by default granted to users SYS and SYSTEM.

Managing privileges is made easier by using roles, which are named groups of related privileges. You create roles, grant system and object privileges to the roles, and then grant roles to users. You can also grant roles to other roles. Unlike schema objects, roles are not contained in any schema.

Oracle Database 12c adds additional administrative privileges including SYSBACKUP, SYSDG, SYSRAC, and SYSKM to enable database backups, Data Guard administration, key management, and RAC management, respectively. With these targeted privileges, one or more administrators can perform all of the normal operations to manage a database without needing the all-powerful SYSDBA privilege.

User privileges provide a basic level of database security.

They are designed to control user access to data and to limit the kinds of SQL statements that users can execute. When creating a user, you grant privileges to enable the user to connect to the database, to run queries and make updates, to create schema objects, and more.

Previously all Oracle DBA-related activities were either performed using the powerful SYSDBA or the SYSOPER role. In support of the SOD requirements starting with Oracle 12c, new administrative roles have been introduced to conform to the principle of access to the least privilege.

Three new users SYSBACKUP, SYSDG and SYSKM are created in support of this, when the database is created, with their account in the "EXPIRED & LOCKED" status. An equivalent administrative privilege with the same name as the user is created as well.

```
SQL>SELECT username, account_status

FROM dba_users

ORDER BY created;

USERNAME ACCOUNT_STATUS

---------------------- ------------------

SYS OPEN

SYSTEM OPEN

SYSKM EXPIRED & LOCKED

SYSDG EXPIRED & LOCKED

SYSBACKUP EXPIRED & LOCKED
```

New Administrative Privileges

These new accounts have been provisioned for use with the appropriate privileges.

```
SQL>SELECT *

FROM V$pwfile_users;

USERNAME SYSDB SYSOP SYSAS SYSBA SYSDG SYSKM CON_ID

------------------------------ ----- ----- ----- ----- -

SYS TRUE TRUE FALSE FALSE FALSE FALSE 0

SYSDG FALSE FALSE FALSE FALSE TRUE FALSE 1

SYSBACKUP FALSE FALSE FALSE TRUE FALSE FALSE 1

SYSKM FALSE FALSE FALSE FALSE FALSE TRUE 1
```

SYSBACKUP will be used to perform all backup and recovery-related operations either via RMAN or SQL*PLUS. Here you can find a complete list of SYSBACKUP privileges you are assigned to when logged in with the SYSBACKUP administrative privilege. SYSDG is in place to separate the Data Guard-related operations from other activities. In addition, you can find a complete list of SYSDG privileges you are assigned to when logged in with the SYSDG administrative privilege.

SYSKM will be responsible for all TDE (Transparent Data Encryption)- and Data Vault-related administrative operations. Here you can find a complete list of SYSKM privileges you are assigned to when logged in with the SYSKM administrative privilege.

None of these new database roles can be dropped. They have enough privileges that by using them a user can connect to the database even if it is closed. In addition, all of these roles are incorporated into the Oracle Database Vault. Actions performed using these privileges can be audited if AUDIT_SYS_OPERATIONS is set to true.

Add New Privileges to a Password File

When a user needs to connect to the database using the SYSBACKUP, SYSDG, or SYSKM administrative privilege, the user must be added to the password file with the appropriate user privilege flag. The option to include these new privileges has been added to the orapwd utility.

orapwd file=[fname] entries=[users] force=[y/n] asm=[y/n] dbuniquename=[dbname] format=[legacy/12] sysbackup=[y/n] sysdg=[y/n] syskm=[y/n] delete=[y/n] input_file=[input-fname] orapwd FILE='$ORACLE_HOME/dbs/orapwvstdb01' ENTRIES=10 SYSBACKUP=y

Current Schema and Session for SYSBACKUP, SYSDG and SYSKM

When a user is connected using any of these admin privileges, the schema that they are assigned to is the SYS schema, and the session name corresponds to the privilege name that they are using.

```
SQL> conn sys as sysdba

Enter password:

Connected.
SQL> select sys_context('userenv', 'current_schema')
current_schema, sys_context('userenv', 'session_user')
session_user from dual;

CURRENT_SCHEMA SESSION_USER

---------------------------- ----------------------------

SYS SYS

SQL> conn sysdg as sysdg

Enter password:

Connected.
SQL> select sys_context('userenv', 'current_schema')
current_schema, sys_context('userenv', 'session_user')
session_user from dual;

CURRENT_SCHEMA SESSION_USER

---------------------------- ----------------------------

SYS SYSDG
```

```
SQL> conn sysbackup as sysbackup

Enter password:

Connected.

SQL> select sys_context('userenv', 'current_schema')
current_schema, sys_context('userenv', 'session_user')
session_user from dual;

CURRENT_SCHEMA SESSION_USER

------------------------------ ------------------------------

SYS SYSBACKUP

SQL> conn syskm as syskm

Enter password:

Connected.

SQL> select sys_context('userenv', 'current_schema')
current_schema, sys_context('userenv', 'session_user')

session_user from dual;

CURRENT_SCHEMA SESSION_USER

------------------------------ ------------------------------

SYSKM SYSKM

    New Database Role OS Group
```

To further ensure the separation of access to the new SYSBACKUP, SYSDG and SYSKM privileges, Oracle recommends mapping them to the new OSBACKUPDBA, OSDGDBA and OSKMDBA operating system groups, respectively.

With the introduction of the new DBA users and the scaled-down privileges, implementing segregation of duties is indeed possible. Further, by providing the flexibility to only assign the required DBA privilege and mapping it to the specific OS role groups, accountability on the use of the specific role is made easier.

About Oracle Database Vault

The Oracle Database Vault security controls protect application data from unauthorised access and comply with privacy and regulatory requirements. We can deploy controls to block privileged account access to application data and control sensitive operations inside the database using trusted path authorization. Through the analysis of privileges and roles, you can increase the security of existing applications by using least privilege best practices. Oracle Database Vault secures existing database environments transparently, eliminating costly and time-consuming application changes.

How Oracle Database Vault Protects Privileged User Accounts

Many security breaches, both external and internal, target privileged users' database accounts to steal data from databases. Oracle Database Vault protects against compromised privileged user account attacks by using realms, factors, and command rules. Combined, these provide powerful security tools to help secure access to databases, applications, and sensitive information. You can combine rules and factors to control the conditions under which commands in the database are allowed to execute and to control access to data protected by a realm. For example, you can create rules and factors to control access to data based on IP addresses, the time of day, and specific programs. These can limit access to only those connections that pass these conditions. This can prevent unauthorised access to application data and access to the database by unauthorised applications.

Oracle Database Vault provides built-in factors that you can use in combination with rules to control access to the database, realm-protected applications, and commands within the database.

You can associate rules and factors with many SQL statements in the database to provide stronger internal controls within the database. You can customise these to meet the operational policies for your site. For example, you could define a rule to limit the execution of the ALTER SYSTEM statement to a specific IP address and hostname.

How Oracle Database Vault Allows for Flexible Security Policies

Oracle Database Vault helps you design flexible security policies for your database.

For example, any database user who has the DBA role can make modifications to basic parameters in a database. Suppose an inexperienced administrator who has system privileges decides to start a new redo log file but does not realise that doing so at a particular time may cause problems for the database. With Oracle Database Vault, you can create a command rule to prevent this user from making such modifications by limiting his or her usage of the ALTER SYSTEM SWITCH LOGFILE statement. Furthermore, you can attach rule sets to the command rule to restrict activity further, such as limiting the statement's execution in the following ways:

☐ by time (for example, only during 4 p.m. and 5 p.m. on Friday afternoons),
☐ by local access only, that is, not remotely and
☐ by IP address (for example, allowing the action to only a specified range of IP addresses).

We can customise Oracle Database Vault separation of duties to fit the requirements of a business of any size. For example, large customers with dedicated IT staff and some outsourced back-end operations can further fine-tune separation of duties to control what outsourced database administrators can do. For smaller organizations with some users handling multiple responsibilities, separation of duties can be tuned down, and these users can create separate dedicated accounts for each responsibility. This helps such users keep track of all actions made and prevents intruders from exploiting compromised privileged database accounts to steal sensitive data. In addition, it allows auditors to verify compliance.

How Oracle Database Vault Addresses Database Consolidation Concerns

Consolidation and cloud environments reduce cost but can expose sensitive application data to those without a true need-to-know.

Data from one country may be hosted in an entirely different country, but access to that data must be restricted based on regulations of the country to which the data belongs.

Oracle Database Vault controls provide increased security for these environments by preventing database administrators from accessing the data of applications. In addition, controls can be used to help block application bypass and enforce a trusted-path from the application tier to the application data.

Oracle Database Vault provides four distinct separations of duty controls for security administration:

- Day-to-day database administrator tasks using the default Oracle Database DBA role,
- Security administrator tasks using the DV_OWNER and DV_ADMIN roles,
- Account administrator tasks using the DV_ACCTMGR role and
- Grants of roles and privileges by a named trusted user.

Oracle Database Vault separation of duty controls can be customised, and organizations with limited resources can assign multiple Oracle Database Vault responsibilities to the same administrator, but using separate accounts for each separation-of-duty role to minimise damage to the database if any one account is stolen and leveraged.

Oracle customers today still have hundreds and even thousands of databases distributed throughout the enterprise and around the world. However, for database consolidation as a cost-saving strategy in the coming years to be effective, the physical security provided by the distributed database architecture must be available in the consolidated environment. Oracle Database Vault addresses the primary security concerns of database consolidation.

- **Administrative privileged account access to application data**: In this case, Oracle Database Vault prevents the DBA from accessing the schemas that are protected by the finance realm. Although the DBA is the most powerful and trusted user, this administrator does not need access to application data residing within the database.
- **Separation of duties for application data access**: In this case, the HR realm owner, created in Oracle Database Vault, has access to the HR realm schemas.

The following figure shows how Oracle Database Vault addresses the following database security concerns:

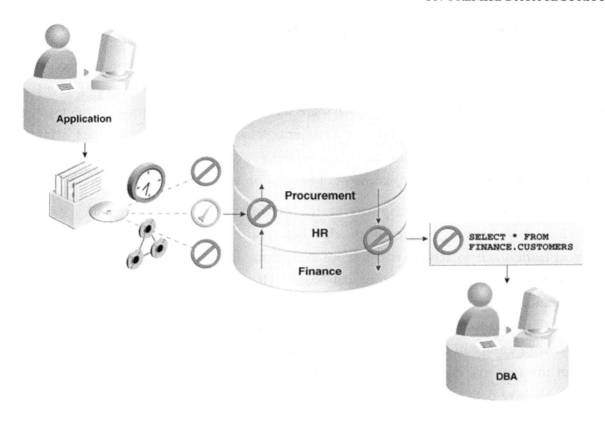

Database consolidation can result in multiple powerful user accounts residing in a single database. This means that in addition to the overall database administrator, individual application schema owners also may have powerful privileges. Revoking some privileges may adversely affect existing applications. Using Oracle Database Vault realms, you can enforce access to applications through a trusted path, preventing database users who have not been specifically authorised access from using powerful privileges to look at other application data. For example, a database administrator who has the SELECT ANY TABLE system privilege can be prevented from using that privilege to view other application data residing in the same database.

Data needs role-based access to improve securing data. It is important to ensure those features to limit the user. By using the feature of SYSBACKUP, SYSDG and SYSKM will do this job. Use the feature of Oracle Vault to ensure these.

DATA ENCRYPTION AND KEY MANAGEMENT

Encryption is nothing but using algorithms to encode data as cipher text. Deception is the process of converting cipher text into original data. Thanks to key management to obtain this process. Data encryption keys are an essential part of any data encryption strategy, because, with the encryption keys, encrypted data can return to its original unencrypted state. An encryption key management system includes generation, exchange, storage, use, destruction, and replacement of encryption keys.

Most of the hacking happens in the network layer during the data transfer. Therefore, it is necessary to encrypt the data before it transmits. Thankfully, we have the support from oracle to achieve it. There we understood the necessity of encrypting data in the database itself before the store database itself, and also we need to ensure the maintenance of original data. With these concepts, we can ensure the data is secure. We usually allow a specific user to access our data in an organization. In addition, it is important to ensure in case of any external persons hacked the data; he needs the key to decrypt the sensitive data. These concepts are achieved by using TDE. Also, we need to ensure sensitive data is not viewed by all of the users in an organization itself like credit card, aadhar card details, etc. Those concepts were achieved with the help of Data Redaction and data masking.

Transparent Data Encryption (TDE)

TDE is the advance data encryption, which is provided b Oracle Database. The base idea is about securing data against security attach. It will help only authorised people able to read data. Use encryption to protect sensitive data in an unprotected environment, such as data you placed on backup tapes that are sent to outside company premises. We can encrypt individual columns in a database table or you can encrypt an entire tablespace, so that it will not be able to read the data without the wallet password, which will always help secure data. Using TDE, we do not need to modify your applications. TDE enables our applications to continue working seamlessly as before.

It automatically encrypts data when it is written to disk and decrypts when we read your applications access it. The key management is built-in, eliminating the complex task of managing and securing encryption keys. Use encryption to protect sensitive data in an unprotected environment, such as data you placed on backup tapes that are sent to outside company premises.

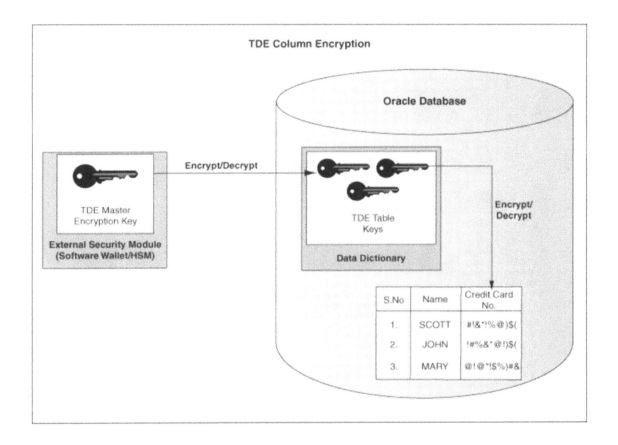

Image: Table Level Encryption

Encrypting data includes the following components:

An algorithm to encrypt the data: Oracle Databases use the encryption algorithm to encrypt and decrypt data. Oracle Database supports several industry-standard encryption and hashing algorithms, including the Advanced Encryption Standard (AES) encryption algorithm.

A key to encrypt and decrypt data: When you encrypt data, Oracle Database uses the key and plain text data as input into the encryption algorithm. When you decrypt data, the key is used as input into the algorithm to reverse the process and retrieve the clear text data. Oracle Database uses a symmetric encryption key to perform this task, in which the same key is used to both encrypt and decrypt the data. The encryption key is stored in the data dictionary, but encrypted with another master key.

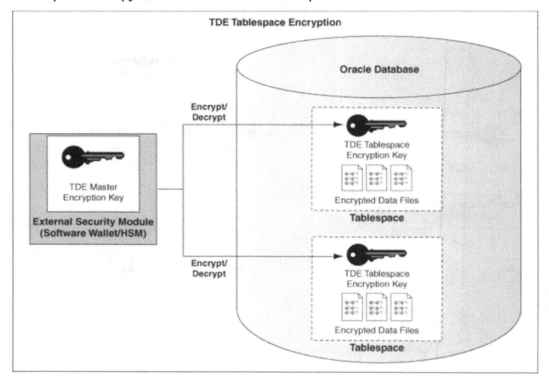

Image: Table Space level Encrypt/Decrypt

How TDE Works:

TDE enables to encrypt individual table columns or an entire tablespace.

When a user inserts data into an encrypted column, TDE encryption automatically encrypts the data. When authorised users select the column, then the data is automatically decrypted. To encrypt data by using TDE, we need to create the following components:

A keystore to store the master encryption key: The keystore is an operating system file that is located outside the database. The database uses the keystore to store the master encryption key. To create the keystore, you can use the ADMINISTER KEY MANAGEMENT SQL statement.

The keystore is encrypted using a password as the encryption key. You create the password when you create the keystore. Access to the contents (or master key) of the keystore is then restricted to only those who know the password. After the keystore is created, you must open the keystore using the password so that the database can access the master encryption key. You can use either software keystores or hardware keystores. A software keystore is defined in a file that you create in a directory location. The software keystore can be one of the following types:

Password-based keystores: Password-based keystores are protected by using a password that you create. You must open the keystore before the keys can be retrieved or used.

Auto-login keystores: Auto-login keystores are protected by a system-generated password and do not need to be explicitly opened by a security administrator. Auto-login keystores are automatically opened when accessed.

Auto-login keystores can be used across different systems. If your environment does not require the extra security provided by a keystore that must be explicitly opened for use, then you can use an auto-login keystore.

Location for keystore: sqlnet.ora file having the location information about keystore.

Oracle DB performs below steps when a user enters data:

1. Retrieve information MasterKey from keystore,
2. Decrypt they encryption key using Masterkey,
3. EncryptionKey uses to encrypt the user-entered data and
4. Stores the data in encryption format in the database.

TDE has the following benefits:

As a security administrator, we can say sure that sensitive data is safe if the storage media or data file is stolen or lost.

Implementing TDE helps to address security-related regulatory compliance issues.

Data from tables is transparently decrypted for the database user. We do not need to create triggers or views to decrypt data.

Database users do not need to be aware that the data they are accessing is stored in encrypted form.

Data is transparently decrypted for the database users and does not require any action on their part.

Applications need not be modified to handle encrypted data. Data encryption and decryption are managed by the database.

Let us See How to Configure TDE:

1. Create Keystore/Wallet Creation:

```
mkdir -p /usr/tmp/WALLET
```

2. Update Wallet Location in sqlnet.ora

```
cat $ORACLE_HOME/network/admin/sqlnet.ora

# sqlnet.ora Network Configuration File:
/home/oracle/app/oracle/product/12.1.0/dbhome_1/network/admin
/sqlnet.ora

# Generated by Oracle configuration tools.

NAMES.DIRECTORY_PATH= (TNSNAMES, EZCONNECT)

ENCRYPTION_WALLET_LOCATION =

(SOURCE =(METHOD = FILE)(METHOD_DATA =

(DIRECTORY = /usr/tmp/WALLET)))
```

3. Create Keystore:

```
SQL> ADMINISTER KEY MANAGEMENT CREATE KEYSTORE
'/usr/tmp/WALLET/' IDENTIFIED BY walletpass#123;

keystore altered.

SQL> host ls /usr/tmp/WALLET/

ewallet.p12
```

4. Open Keystore:

```
SQL> ADMINISTER KEY MANAGEMENT SET KEYSTORE OPEN
IDENTIFIED BY walletpass#123;

keystore altered.
```

5. Activate the Key:

```
SQL> SET LINESIZE 100

SELECT con_id, key_id FROM v$encryption_keys;SQL>

no rows selected

SQL> ADMINISTER KEY MANAGEMENT SET KEY IDENTIFIED BY
walletpass#123 WITH BACKUP;

keystore altered.

SQL> SET LINESIZE 100

SELECT con_id, key_id FROM v$encryption_keys;SQL>

CON_ID KEY_ID

---------- ---------------------------------------------------
--------------------------

0 AS6cSkI4u09zv9+RRWMrX2QAAAAAAAAAAAAAAAAAAAAAAAAAAA

SQL> SET LINESIZE 200

COLUMN wrl_parameter FORMAT A50
```

```
SELECT * FROM v$encryption_wallet;

SQL> SQL>

WRL_TYPE    WRL_PARAMETER STATUS  WALLET_TYPE

-------------------- ------------------------------------------

---------- -------------

WALLET_OR        FULLY_BAC CON_ID

------------------        --------- --------- ----------

FILE /usr/tmp/WALLET/ OPEN  PASSWORD   SINGLE NO 0
```

6. Create an encrypted tablespace:

```
SQL> CREATE TABLESPACE TEST_ENCRY

datafile '/home/oracle/app/oracle/oradata/cdb1/testencry.dbf'
size 2G

ENCRYPTION USING 'AES256'

DEFAULT STORAGE(ENCRYPT);

Tablespace created.

SQL> create table emp_ency(

empno Number(3),

Name varchar(10)

) tablespace TEST_ENCRY;

Table created

SQL> select tablespace_name,encrypted from dba_tablespaces
where tablespace_name='TEST_ENCRY';

TABLESPACE_NAME   ENC

----------------------------- ---

TEST_ENCRY        YES
```

7. Create table with an encrypted column:

```
SQL> CREATE TABLE employee (

first_name VARCHAR2(128),

last_name VARCHAR2(128),

empID NUMBER,

salary NUMBER(6) ENCRYPT

);

Table created.

SQL> select owner,table_name,column_name,encryption_alg from
dba_encrypted_columns where table_name='EMPLOYEE';

OWNER  TABLE_NAME COLUMN_NAME ENCRYPTION_A

---------- ------------ ------------ ------------

HR     EMPLOYEE SALARY  AES 192 bits

Enable Auto-Login:

SQL> SELECT * FROM v$encryption_wallet;

WRL_TYPE   WRL_PARAMETER STATUS WALLET_TYPE WALLET_OR

------------------- ----------------------------------------

------------ ---------- ----

FULLY_BAC CON_ID

---------- --------------

FILE       /usr/tmp/WALLET/    OPEN PASSWORD SINGLE NO 0
```

Here the wallet_type is PASSWORD, so every time we restart the database, we always need to open the key/wallet. To avoid this, we can enable auto-login, so that next time when DB gets restarted, the wallet opens automatically.

```
SQL> ADMINISTER KEY MANAGEMENT CREATE AUTO_LOGIN KEYSTORE
FROM KEYSTORE '/usr/tmp/WALLET/' IDENTIFIED BY
walletpass#123;

keystore altered.

SQL> SELECT * FROM v$encryption_wallet;

WRL_TYPE WRL_PARAMETER STATUS    WALLET_TYPE      WALLET_OR
FULLY_BAC CON_ID

-------- ------------------ -------    ------------- ----------
----------- ---------

FILE /usr/tmp/WALLET/ OPEN   PASSWORD   SINGLE NO           0

SQL>

SQL> startup force

ORACLE instance started.

Total System Global Area 838860800 bytes

Fixed Size 2929936 bytes

Variable Size 570428144 bytes

Database Buffers 260046848 bytes

Redo Buffers 5455872 bytes

Database mounted.

Database opened.

SQL> SELECT * FROM v$encryption_wallet;

WRL_TYPE WRL_PARAMETER STATUS    WALLET_TYPE      WALLET_OR
FULLY_BAC CON_ID

--------- ------------------ ------- ------------- ----------

FILE /usr/tmp/WALLET/ OPEN AUTO-LOGIN SINGLE NO 0
```

Now we are able to view **Wallet_type from password to auto-login.**

NOTE: To create a keystore, a user should have either ADMINISTER KEY MANAGEMENT or SYSKM privilege.

Related dictionary tables for TDE:

----What tables contain TDE encrypted columns?

```
sql> select table_name, column_name from dba_encrypted_columns;
```

-------What tables are stored in TDE encrypted tablespaces?

```
sql> select a.table_name, a.tablespace_name from dba_tables a,
dba_tablespaces b
where a.tablespace_name = b.tablespace_name and b.encrypted =
'YES';
```

-------What indexes are stored in TDE encrypted tablespaces?

```
sql> select a.index_name, a.tablespace_name from dba_indexes a,
dba_tablespaces b
where a.tablespace_name = b.tablespace_name and b.encrypted =
'YES' and index_name not like 'SYS_IL%';
```

-------Getting key/wallet details:

```
SQL> SELECT * FROM v$encryption_wallet;
SQL> SELECT con_id, key_id FROM v$encryption_keys;
```

Oracle Data Redaction

Oracle Data Redaction provides the ability to mask data, typically sensitive data in real-time like a credit card, aadhar card details, etc. before displaying with the application. For example, in a call centre, an agent is able to view sensitive data in application because of the data he/she gets from PROD. That exposition may lead to privacy regulation and the corresponding user into risk.

Oracle Advanced Security Data Redaction is on-the-fly redaction, i.e., masking of sensitive data in query results prior to display by applications, as shown in the following illustration. It enables consistent redaction of database columns across application modules accessing the same data.

Data Redaction minimises changes because it does not alter source data in internal database buffers, caches, or storage, and it preserves the original data type and formatting when transformed data is returned to the application.

Data Redaction is easy to deploy because of its transparency to applications and the database. Data Redaction supports the column data types that are frequently used by applications and various database objects, including tables, views, and materialised views. Redacted values retain key characteristics of the original data, such as the data type and optional formatting characters. For transparency to the database, Data Redaction does not affect administrative tasks such as data movement using Oracle Data Pump or database backup and restore using Oracle Recovery Manager. It does not interfere with database cluster configurations such as Oracle Real Application Clusters, Oracle Active Data Guard, and Oracle GoldenGate.

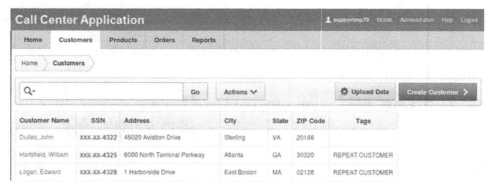

In the traditional method, we need third-party software, but Data Redaction directly enforces in kernel across the application. A redaction position library gives pre-configured segment layouts to browse for normal sorts of delicate data, for example, Visa numbers and national recognisable proof numbers. Once empowered, polices are authorised quickly, notwithstanding for dynamic sessions.

Data Redaction Policies and Transformations

Data Redaction underpins various changes that can redact all data in indicated segments, protect certain bits of the data, or arbitrarily produce substitution data. Instances of the upheld data changes appear in the accompanying representation.

Data Redaction can be connected specifically, in view of explanatory approach conditions that use the runtime settings accessible from the database and from the running application. Models incorporate client identifiers, client jobs, and customer IP addresses. Setting data accessible from Oracle Application Express (APEX), Oracle Real Application Security, and Oracle Label Security additionally can be used.

Redacting APEX applications is direct in light of the fact that arrangement conditions can utilise the application clients and application identifiers that APEX naturally tracks. Different runtime conditions can be combined inside a Data Redaction arrangement for fine-grained power over when redaction happens.

Redaction approaches are put away and oversaw inside the database, and they go live quickly after being empowered. Superficially, Data Redaction and Oracle Data Masking appear to be very comparable. In any case, there is a significant distinction in that Oracle Data Redaction does not physically change the put-away data. Accordingly, Oracle Data Redaction bolsters a subset of the changes accessible with Oracle Data Masking. The intensity of Data Redaction lives in its unrivalled exhibition, requirement inside the database bit, and the explanatory strategy conditions.

The sorts of redaction that you can perform are explained as follows:

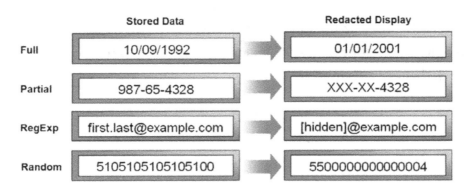

Full redaction: You redact the majority of the substance of the section data. The redacted worth that is come back to the questioning client relies upon the data sort of the segment. For instance, sections of the NUMBER data type are redacted with a zero (0), and character data types are redacted with a clear space.

Partial redaction: You redact a bit of the section data. For instance, you can redact the majority of a Social Security Number with reference marks (*), aside from the last four digits.

Regular expressions: You can utilise regular expressions in both full and partial redaction. This empowers you to redact data dependent on a quest design for the data. For instance, you can utilise regular expressions to redact explicit telephone numbers or email addresses in your data.

Random redaction: The redacted data exhibited to the questioning client shows up as randomly created qualities each time it is shown, contingent upon the data kind of the section.

No redaction: This choice empowers you to test the inner activity of your redaction strategies, with no impact on the consequences of questions against tables with arrangements characterised by them. You can utilise this choice to test the redaction arrangement definitions before applying them to a generation domain.

Data Redaction plays out the redaction at runtime, that is, the minute that the client attempts to see the data. This usefulness is in a perfect world appropriate for dynamic generation frameworks in which data always shows signs of change. While the data is being redacted, Oracle Database can process the majority of the data normally and to save the back-end referential honesty limitations. Data Redaction can assist you with complying with industry guidelines, for example, Payment Card Industry Data Security Standard (PCI DSS) and the Sarbanes-Oxley Act.

Steps to Deploy Data Redaction

Data Redaction can be obtained in two ways: using OEM (Oracle Enterprise Manager) and API (PL/SQL Procedure) to a specific column, transformation types, and conditions. OEM provides an interface to apply this.

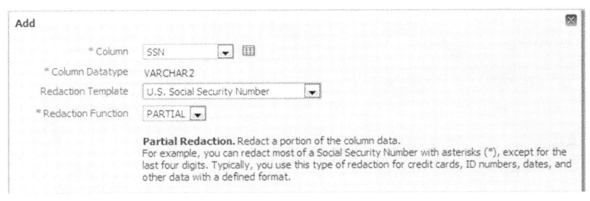

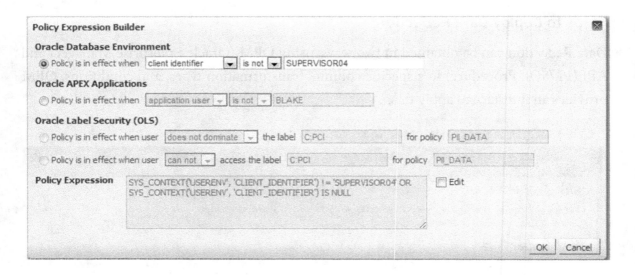

Before moving ahead with Data Redaction, grant execute object-level privilege on package dbms_redact to the user.

sqlplus / as sysdba

grant execute on dbms_redact to scott;

Applying redaction policy without filtering, i.e., expression => '1=1'. It means this redaction policy will be applied to all of the users and roles.

```
begin

dbms_redact.add_policy(

object_schema => 'SCOTT',

object_name => 'EMP',

column_name => 'SAL',

policy_name => 'SCOTT_EMP_REDACT',

function_type => DBMS_REDACT.full,

expression => '1=1');

end;
```

/

We can view the default redact value for the numeric data and other data type. Use SQL command below to view.

```
select NUMBER_VALUE from redaction_values_for_type_full;
```

We can update the default redact value with the following command. In this case, we have replaced the default numeric reduction value from 0 to 6.

```
EXEC DBMS_REDACT.UPDATE_FULL_REDACTION_VALUES (number_val =>
6);
```

Restart the database instance to get the change into effect.

We can use the following data dictionaries to view the details of redaction.

```
select * from redaction_policies;
```

```
select * from redaction_columns;
```

Modify an Existing Policy

We need to use ALTER_POLICY procedure to modify an existing redaction policy. Instead of displaying a salary as six, we can hide some digits from the whole column. As per modification below SAL column value will be displayed as 9 for two digits from left. If someone's salary is 2500, then it will be displayed as 9900. The first two digits will be converted to 9.

```
begin
dbms_redact.alter_policy(
object_schema => 'SCOTT',
object_name => 'EMP',
policy_name => 'SCOTT_EMP_REDACT',
action => DBMS_REDACT.modify_column,
column_name => 'SAL',
```

```
    function_type => DBMS_REDACT.partial,

    function_parameters => '9,1,2'

    );

    end;

    /
```

Drop column from the redaction policy.

```
    begin

    dbms_redact.alter_policy(

    object_schema => 'SCOTT',

    object_name => 'EMP',

    policy_name => 'SCOTT_EMP_REDACT',

    action => DBMS_REDACT.drop_column,

    column_name => 'JOB'

    );

    end;

    /
```

Drop redaction policy using drop_policy procedure.

```
begin

dbms_redact.drop_policy(

object_schema => 'SCOTT',

object_name => 'EMP',

policy_name => 'SCOTT_EMP_REDACT');

end;

/
```

Data Masking

We recommend ensuring that data key should be in separate place rather than oracle home. In addition, ensure proper key generated after clone. Also, ensure data is open to read in a lower environment. The above points are important for TDE. The Data Redaction and masking are ensuring that data is not viewed by unauthorised users—more traditional format like disk volume encryption lagging the performance. As we need to encrypt all content including tablespaces, so it is necessary to decrypt at standby database (like redo logs). In case of any failure to apply redo logs, it includes a lot of time and annual effort. Therefore, we have techniques to eliminate the limitation using oracle features itself.

Protecting Data using Oracle Maximum Availability Architecture

When considering security, it is important to ensure availability. High data availability is ensured by achieving below key architecture to preventing downtime.

Data availability: Ensure that we are not in interruption business. We need to ensure that data is available.

Data protection: Prevent data loss that compromises the feasibility of the business.

Performance: Ensure better response time for business operations.

Cost: Reduce deployment, management and support cost to conserve corporate resource.

Risk: Consistently achieve required service levels over a long period of time as the business evolves with no costly surprises or disappointments.

This results in cost-effective solutions that reduce business risks and achieve unique levels of data protection, availability, performance, and return on investment. This innovation results in High-Availability solutions that give true competitive advantages to enterprises, by helping them achieve service level objectives for high availability in the most cost-effective manner.

ORACLE MAXIMUM AVAILABILITY ARCHITECTURE (OMAA)

OMAA is nothing but a combination of High Availability integrated with best practices. MAA best practices are maintained by the oracle development team that is continually monitoring and validating the practices. These practices involve servers, network, storage, and Operating Systems, which are continually updated and extended.

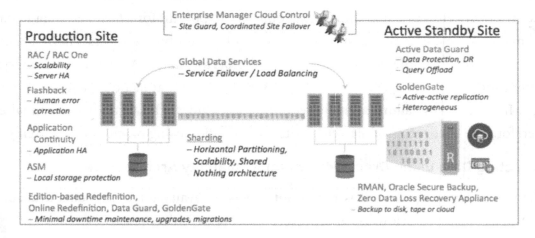

Addressing Unplanned Downtime

As humans, we face health issues which we cannot plan, but we are trying to avoid those by maintaining some hygienic lifestyle. In the same manner, we need to address the application too. For that, we need to maintain some high features, which will ensure and support. The unplanned downtime includes storage error, server error, data availability fail, and human error. MAA mitigates and prevents unplanned downtime with HA concepts.

Let us see how we are able to maintain this concept with the help of oracle products. To support HA, we are going to see the most popular features like RAC, Data Guard, ASM, Oracle Secure Backup, and RMAN.

Multitenant architecture across all Oracle High Availability features new levels of redundancy, transparent failover of in-flight transactions, and zero-data-loss disaster protection at any geographic distance. This represents the next generation in database technology, and long-standing and time-proven Oracle High Availability design principles are ready from day one to provide the extreme availability required by consolidated environments. This feature is enhanced in 18C.

Oracle Sharding is a scalability and availability feature for custom-designed OLTP applications that enables distribution and replication of data across a pool of discrete Oracle Databases. This pool of databases is presented to the application as a single logical database. Applications elastically scale (data, transactions, and users) to any level, on any platform, simply by adding additional databases (shards) to the pool. This feature was introduced from Oracle 12c. Oracle Sharding trades-off transparency in return for massive linear scalability, greater availability, and geographical distribution.

Oracle Sharding provides superior runtime performance and simpler life-cycle management compared to home-grown deployments that use a similar approach to scalability. It also provides the advantages of an enterprise DBMS, including relational schema, SQL, and other programmatic interfaces, support for complex data types, online schema changes, multicore scalability, advanced security, compression, high availability, ACID properties, consistent reads, developer agility with JSON, and much more.

In Oracle Database 18c, user-defined sharding has been introduced which allows you to explicitly specify the mapping of data to individual shards which addresses requirements to store data to a particular shard because of performance or regulatory reasons. In a multitenant environment, single PDB deployment can now be used as a shard or for deploying a shard catalogue. GoldenGate replication is now supported with sharding. To provide better cache utilization and to dramatically reduce block pings across instances, Oracle RAC Sharding in 18c creates an affinity for table partitions to particular

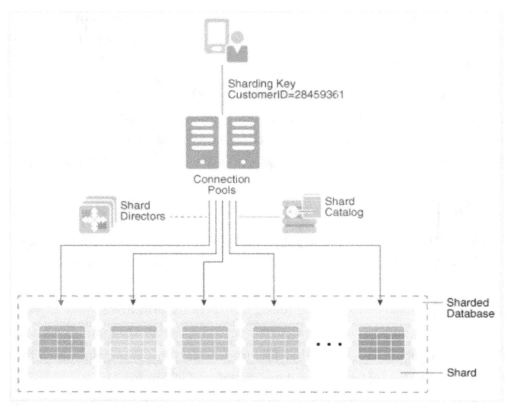

Oracle RAC instances, and routes database requests that specify a partitioning key to the instance that logically holds the corresponding partition. Additional enhancements include multishard query consistency level, optimiser enhancements for multishard queries, and support for JSON, LOBs and spatial objects.

The Oracle MAA sharding solution provides the following features and benefits:

- Fault tolerance with zero points of failure
- Fault isolation in which any shard failure or maintenance has zero or very minimal impact on the overall application and sharded database
- Failover each shard quickly for high local availability or remote disaster recovery
- Apply changes online, in a rolling manner, or switch over to an upgraded shard, with zero or minimal downtime for planned maintenance activities
- Migrate, split, and rebalance existing shards with zero or minimal application impact

☐ Grow and scale the application by adding shards with zero or minimal application impact

☐ Route and load balance across various shards and across geographic regions

☐ Reduce manageability costs with centralised management interface for the sharded database

RAC (*Oracle Real Applications Cluster*) ensures that multiple instances are running across the different servers under a cluster against a shared set of data files. This will improvise application availability to the users/business. The database spans multiple hardware systems and yet appears as a single database to the application.

This architecture extends availability and feasibility to all applications as detailed below:

Fault Tolerance: Within a server pool specifically for hardware failure, because multiple nodes are running, one single node failure will not affect the other nodes. The beauty of this architecture is we can put online/offline other nodes without disturbing remaining nodes, which ensures data availability.

Flexibility and Cost Effectiveness: This is mainly for capacity planning so the system can scale up to business needs without modifying existing systems. This will reduce the cost of future scaling resource for business.

In Oracle Database 12.2, Oracle RAC has improved scalability, availability, and performance. They are achieved using service-oriented buffer cache access, pluggable database and service isolations and near-zero downtime reconfigurations.

Massive parallel query RACs can be obtained by overlaying Hadoop Cluster (HDFS) with an Oracle Flex Cluster to access data in Hadoop via SQL and perform cross-data analysis. Moreover, you can use read-only workloads on read-mostly leaf node instances (RAC Reader Nodes) that can be scaled to hundreds of nodes with no delay in accessing updated data and without affecting the OLTP performance.

Node Weighting is another new feature in Oracle Database 12.2 that considers the workload hosted in the cluster during fencing operation by letting the majority of the work to survive in the event where everything else is equal. Autonomous Health Framework continuously monitors and analyses and is hosted on a Domain Service Cluster (DSC) instead of the production cluster. DSC is also used for Rapid Home Provisioning; Oracle RAC also supports the multitenant architecture, and in addition to providing server HA, Oracle RAC software stack2 is the ideal shared infrastructure for database consolidation.

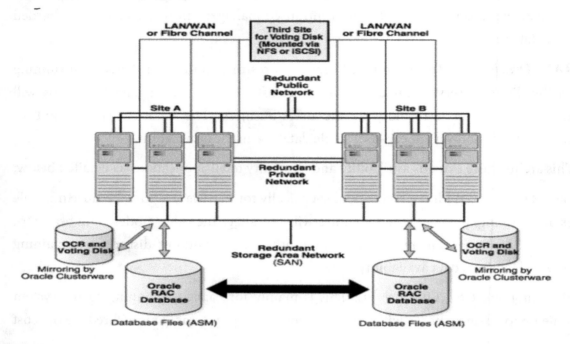

Oracle RAC is the recommended MAA best practice for server HA.

RAC One Node, however, is an acceptable lower-cost alternative to Oracle RAC, if a slightly lesser level of HA is acceptable and scalability is not a requirement.

RAC One Node is an active-passive failover technology. While it is built upon the same infrastructure as Oracle RAC, RAC One Node has only one database instance open at a time during normal operation. If the server hosting the open instance fails, RAC One Node automatically starts a new database instance on a second node to quickly resume service.

RAC One Node provides several advantages over alternative active-passive clustering technologies. In a RAC One Node configuration, Oracle Database HA Services, Grid Infrastructure, and database listeners are always running on the second node. At failover time, only the database instance and database services need to start, improving availability by reducing the time required to resume service.

RAC One Node also provides the same advantages for planned maintenance as Oracle RAC. RAC One Node allows two active database instances during periods of planned maintenance to allow graceful migration of users from one node to another with zero downtime. Maintenance is performed in a rolling manner across nodes, while database services remain available to users at all times.

Oracle Database with Oracle Data Guard: With the help of Data Guard, we can obtain a very fast failover in automatic during the database, node, and media corruption failures. The traditional high-availability solutions like Tape backup and Recovery may help, but time is of the essence to ensure HA. The Data Guard can be used in read-only mode so that it can be used for reporting purposes.

Oracle Data Guard Advantages Over Traditional Solutions

Oracle Data Guard provides a number of advantages over traditional solutions, including the following:

- Fast, automatic or automated database failover for data corruptions, lost writes, and database and site failures
- Automatic corruption repair automatically replaces a corrupted block on the primary or physical standby by copying a good block from a physical standby or primary database
- Most comprehensive protection against data corruptions and lost writes on the primary database
- Reduced downtime for storage, Oracle ASM, Oracle RAC, system migrations, some platform migrations, and changes using Data Guard switchover
- Reduced downtime with Oracle Data Guard rolling upgrade capabilities
- Ability to off-load primary database activities—such as backups, queries, or reporting—without sacrificing the RTO and RPO ability to use the standby database as a read-only resource using the real-time query applying lag capability

- Ability to integrate non-database files using Oracle Database File System (DBFS) as part of the full site failover operations
- No need for instance restart, storage remastering, or application reconnections after site failures
- Transparency to applications
- Transparent and integrated support for application failover
- Effective network utilization

For data resident in Oracle databases, Oracle Data Guard, with its built-in zero-data-loss capability, is more efficient, less expensive, and better optimised for data protection and disaster recovery than traditional remote mirroring solutions. Oracle Data Guard provides a compelling set of technical and business reasons that justify its adoption as the disaster recovery and data protection technology of choice, over traditional remote mirroring solutions.

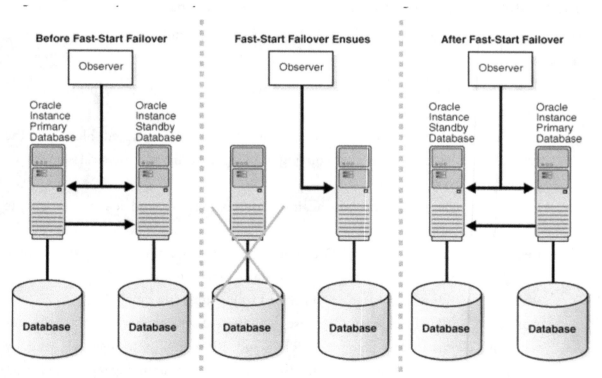

Oracle Data Guard Advantages vs Remote Mirroring Solutions

The following list summarises the advantages of using Oracle Data Guard compared to using remote mirroring solutions:

- **Better network efficiency**: With Oracle Data Guard, only the redo data needs to be sent to the remote site, and the redo data can be compressed to provide even greater network efficiency. However, if a remote mirroring solution is used for data protection, typically, you must mirror the database files, the online redo log, the archived redo logs, and the control file. If the fast recovery area is on the source volume that is remotely mirrored, then you must also remotely mirror the flashback logs. Thus, compared to Oracle Data Guard, a remote mirroring solution must transmit each change many more times to the remote site.

- **Better performance**: Oracle Data Guard only transmits write I/Os to the redo log files of the primary database, whereas remote mirroring solutions must transmit these writes and every write I/O to data files, additional members of online log file groups, archived redo log files, and control files.

Oracle Data Guard is designed so that it does not affect the Oracle database writer (DBWR) process that writes to data files, because anything that slows down the DBWR process affects database performance. However, remote mirroring solutions affect the DBWR process performance because they subject all the DBWR process write I/Os to network and disk I/O-induced delays inherent to synchronous, zero-data-loss configurations.

Compared to mirroring, Oracle Data Guard provides better performance and is more efficient. Oracle Data Guard always verifies the state of the standby database and validates the data before applying redo data, and Oracle Data Guard enables you to use the standby database for updates while it protects the primary database.

- **Better suited for WANs**: Remote mirroring solutions based on storage systems often have a distance limitation due to the underlying communication technology (Fibre Channel or ESCON (Enterprise Systems Connection)) used by the storage systems. In a typical example, the maximum distance between the systems connected in a point-to-point fashion and running synchronously can be only 10 kilometres. By using specialised devices, this distance can be extended to 66 kilometres. However, when the datacentres are located more than 66 kilometres apart, you must use a series of repeaters and converters from third-party vendors. These devices convert an ESCON or a Fibre Channel to the appropriate IP, ATM, or SONET networks.

☐ **Better resilience and data protection**: Oracle Data Guard ensures much better data protection and data resilience than remote mirroring solutions. This is because corruption introduced on the production database probably can be mirrored by remote mirroring solutions to the standby site, but corruption is eliminated by Oracle Data Guard.

For example, if a stray write occurs to a disk, or there is a corruption in the file system, or the host bus adaptor corrupts a block as it is written to disk, then a remote mirroring solution may propagate this corruption to the disaster-recovery site. Because Oracle Data Guard only propagates the redo data in the logs, and the log file consistency is checked before it is applied, all such external corruptions are eliminated by Oracle Data Guard. Automatic block repair may be possible, thus eliminating any downtime in an Oracle Data Guard configuration.

☐ **Higher flexibility**: Oracle Data Guard is implemented on pure commodity hardware. It requires only a standard TCP/IP-based network link between the two computers. There is no fancy or expensive hardware required. It also allows the storage to be laid out in a different fashion from the primary computer. For example, you can put the files on different disks, volumes, file systems, and so on.

☐ **Better functionality**: Oracle Data Guard provides a full suite of data protection features that provide a much more comprehensive and effective solution optimised for data protection and disaster recovery than remote mirroring solutions. For example: Active Data Guard, Redo Apply for physical standby databases, and SQL Apply for logical standby databases, multiple protection modes, push-button automated switchover and failover capabilities, automatic gap detection and resolution, GUI-driven management and monitoring framework, and cascaded redo log destinations.

☐ **Higher ROI**: Businesses must obtain maximum value from their IT investments, and ensure that no IT infrastructure is sitting idle. Oracle Data Guard is designed to allow businesses to get something useful out of their expensive investment in a disaster-recovery site. Typically, this is not possible with remote mirroring solutions.

Oracle Active Data Guard

This allows a physical standby database to be open read-only while changes are applied to it from the primary database. It enables read-only applications to use the standby with minimal latency between the data on the standby and that on the primary database, even while processing very high transaction volumes at the primary database. This is sometimes referred to as **a real-time query**.

An Oracle Active Data Guard standby database is used for automatic repair of data corruption detected by the primary database, transparent to the application. In the event of an unplanned outage on the primary database, high availability is maintained by quickly failing over to the standby database. An Active Data Guard standby database can also be used to off-load fast incremental backups from the primary database given that it is a block-for-block physical replica of the primary.

Benefits of Oracle Active Data Guard

An Oracle Active Data Guard

☐ Makes productive use of existing physical standby databases
☐ Improves primary database performance by offloading processing to the standby database
☐ Improves backup performance by offloading fast incremental backups from the primary database to an active standby
☐ Allows the active standby to automatically repair block corruptions detected at the primary database, transparent to the user and application (and vice versa)
☐ Provides real-time data access for reporting

- ☐ Provides real-time data for Business Intelligence, EPM, and Oracle Exadata
- ☐ Offers flexible options to scale read performance while still maintaining disaster recovery, through Reader Farms

Role Transitions

Role transition feature is available in Oracle Enterprise Edition.

An Oracle Database operates in one of two roles: primary or standby. Using Oracle Data Guard, you can change the role of a database using either a switchover or a failover operation.

A switchover is a role reversal between the primary database and one of its standby databases. A switchover ensures no data loss. This is typically done for planned maintenance of the primary system. During a switchover, the primary database transitions to a standby role, and the standby database transitions to the primary role.

A failover is when the primary database is unavailable. Failover is performed only in the event of a failure of the primary database, and the failover results in a transition of a standby database to the primary role.

Role Transitions Options	RTO	RPO
Switchover	30 min	0 loss (zero)
Failover	15–20 min	Minimal loss ~5–10 min

Role Transitions Options	Standard Edition	Enterprise Edition
Switchover	Y	Y
Failover	N	Y

Recommendations and Pre-Requirement for Configuring Standby

1. Archive log mode should be enabled
2. All tables should be in logging mode

3. Force Logging should be enabled at the database level
4. Operating System Patch level should be the same
5. Oracle Binary Patch set level should be the same
6. Archive log space should be the same as production destination space
7. Primary and Standby sites require network access

Corruption Prevention, Detection, and Repair

The MAA-recommended way to achieve the most comprehensive data corruption, prevention and detection is to use Oracle Data Guard and configure the DB_BLOCK_CHECKING, DB_BLOCK_CHECKSUM, and DB_LOST_WRITE_PROTECT database initialization parameters on the Data Guard primary and standby databases. The below tools are highly helpful in achieving this.

☐ Oracle Data Guard and Active Data Guard
☐ Data Recovery Advisor
☐ Oracle Flashback
☐ Oracle Recovery Manager (RMAN)
☐ Automatic Diagnostic Recovery (ADR)
☐ Oracle Secure Backup
☐ The MAA Advisor component of OEM Grid Control

When oracle issues write operation, it follows as below I/O sequence.

☐ To file system
☐ To Volume manager
☐ To device driver
☐ To Host Bus Adapter
☐ To Storage Controller
☐ To disk drive where data is stored

Hardware failure or some reasons in any layer may lead to data to writing into the disk. This is known as lost write. Data corruption can be classified into two categories.

Physical Corruption: A block does not have an invalid checksum or header, or when the block contains only zeroes as value, then the database will not be able to consider this as a valid oracle block. So this is known as physical corruptions/media corruption.

Logical Corruption: A block has a valid checksum, but the blocks are logically inconsistent. It happens when below of block header corrupt. In this case, the checksum of a block is correct, but the structure is wrong. This one is known as lost write.

There are two types of block corruptions.

Intrablock corruption: The corruption occurs in the block itself and can be either a physical or logical corruption.

Interblock corruption: The corruption occurs between blocks and can only be a logical corruption.

Oracle Data Guard is the best solution for protecting Oracle data against data loss and corruption, and lost writes. It is the only Oracle feature that maintains one or more standby databases to protect enterprise data against failures, disasters, errors, and data corruptions. With Data Guard, you can deploy and manage one or more standby copies of the primary (production) database in the local datacentre or a remote datacentre. All of the advantages of data protection derive from this fact.

For example, you can use Data Guard to maintain another copy of your data on a standby database that is continuously updated with changes from the production database. Data Guard validates all changes before they are applied to the standby database, preventing physical corruptions from propagating and corrupting the physical standby database. The standby database can be activated if the production database should become unavailable on account of site disasters, data corruption, or human error.

Starting in Oracle Database 11g Release 2 (11.2), the primary database automatically attempts to repair the corrupted block in real-time by fetching a good version of the same block from a physical standby database. Moreover, the Oracle Active Data Guard option, a feature that enables a physical standby database to be opened read-only while Redo Apply is active, is required for automatic block repair. This feature allows corrupt data blocks to be automatically repaired as soon as the corruption is detected.

Backup and Recovery

Backup and recovery are the set of concepts, procedures, and strategies involved in protecting the database against data loss caused by a media failure or user errors. In general, the purpose of a backup and recovery strategy is to protect the database against data loss and reconstruct lost data.

A backup is a copy of data. A backup can include crucial parts of the database such as data files, redo logs, archive logs, the server parameter file, and control file. A sample backup and recovery scenario is a failed disk drive that causes the loss of a data file. If a backup of the lost file exists, then you can restore and recover it—the operations involved in restoring data to its state before the loss is known as media recovery.

Backup and Recovery Techniques

RMAN

RMAN is an Oracle Database utility that integrates with an Oracle Database to perform backup and recovery activities, including maintaining a repository of historical backup metadata in the control file of every database that it backs up. RMAN can also maintain a centralised backup repository called a recovery catalogue in a different database. RMAN is an Oracle Database feature and does not require separate installation.

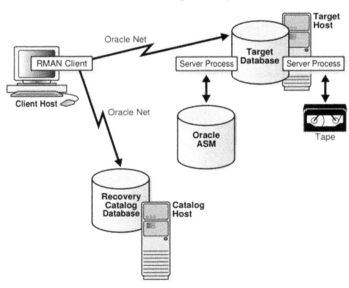

User-Managed techniques

As an alternative to RMAN, you can use operating system commands such as the Linux dd for backing up and restoring files and the SQL*Plus RECOVER command for media recovery. User-managed backup and recovery are fully supported by Oracle, although RMAN is recommended because it is integrated with Oracle Database and simplifies administration.

Types of RMAN Database Backup

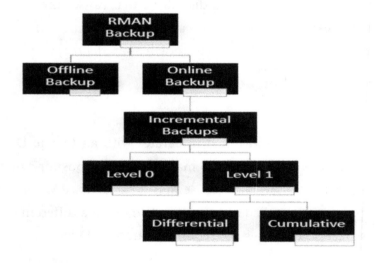

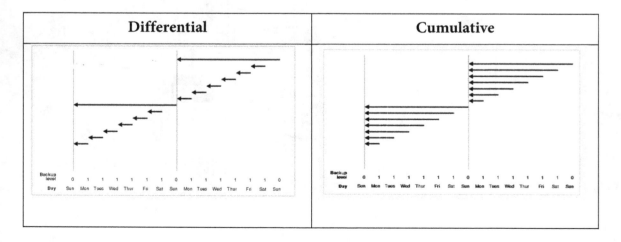

Offline Backup: Offline backups are taken after bringing down the database, mostly taken before database upgrade or any cold maintenance.

Online Backup: Online backups are taken keeping the database up and running. All Mission Critical or production database backup are taken online.

Level 0 & Level 1: "Level 0" incremental backup is the same as a full database backup.

In "Level 1" backup, which contains only blocks changed after a previous incremental backup, if our current database or parent database incarnation does not have the "Level 0" backup, we would directly proceed for "Level 1" and then it'll take automatically to "Level 0". For effective Level 1, Block Change Tracking (BCT) has to be enabled. (BCT can be done only in Enterprise edition).

Cumulative: Includes all block changes since the most recent Level 0 backup.

Differential: Includes only blocks changed since the most recent incremental backup. Incremental backups are differential by default.

RMAN provides the following benefits:

- Automatic channel failover on backup and restore operations
- Automatic failover to a previous backup when the restore operation discovers a missing or corrupt backup
- Automatic creation of new database files and temporary files during recovery
- Automatic recovery through a previous point-in-time recovery—recovery through resetlogs
- Block media recovery, which enables the data file to remain online while fixing the block corruption
- Fast incremental backups using BCT
- Fast backup and restore operations with intrafile and interfile parallelism
- Enhanced security with virtual private catalogue
- Lower space consumption when creating a database over the network by eliminating staging areas
- The merger of incremental backups into image copies in the background, providing up-to-date recoverability

- ☐ Optimised backup and restore of required files only
- ☐ Retention policy to ensure that relevant backups are retained
- ☐ Ability to resume backup and restore of previously failed operations
- ☐ Automatic backup of the control file and the server parameter file, ensuring that backup metadata is available in times of database structural changes and media failure and disasters
- ☐ Online backup that does not require you to place the database into hot backup mode

Oracle Secure Backup

Oracle Secure Backup is a centralised tape backup management solution providing heterogeneous data protection in distributed UNIX, Linux, Windows, and Network Attached Storage (NAS) Environments.

By protecting the file system and Oracle Database data, Oracle Secure Backup provides a complete tape backup solution for your IT environment. Oracle Secure Backup is tightly integrated with RMAN to provide the media management layer for RMAN, supporting releases since Oracle9i. With optimised integration points, Oracle Secure Backup and RMAN provide the fastest and most efficient tape backup capability for Oracle Database.

You can back up distributed servers to local and remote tape devices from a central Oracle Secure Backup administrative server using backup policies, calendar-based scheduling for lights out operations, or on-demand backup for immediate requirements. With its highly scalable client/server architecture, Oracle Secure Backup provides local and remote data protection, using Secure Sockets layer (SSL) for secure intradomain communication and two-way server authentication.

Oracle Secure Backup provides the following benefits:

- ☐ Optimised tape backup for Oracle Database by backing up only the currently used blocks and increasing backup performance by 10% to 25%.
- ☐ Policy-based management that allows backup administrators to exercise precise control over the backup domain.

- Dynamic drive sharing for increased tape resource use.
- Heterogeneous Storage Area Network (SAN) support allowing NAS, UNIX, Windows, and Linux to share tape drives and media.
- File system backup at the file, directory, file system or raw partition level with full, incremental, and offsite backup scheduling.
- Integration with OEM, providing an intuitive, familiar interface.
- Backup encryption to tape.
- Broad tape-device support for new and legacy tape devices in SAN and SCSI environments.
- Network Data Management Protocol (NDMP) support for highly efficient backup of NAS files.
- A scalable, low-cost licensing model that reduces IT costs and operational considerations.

Automatic Storage Management

Oracle ASM provides a vertically integrated file system and volume manager directly in the Oracle Database kernel, resulting in:

- Significantly less work to provision database storage.
- Higher level of availability.
- Elimination of the expense, installation, and maintenance of specialised storage products.
- Unique capabilities for database applications.

For optimal performance, Oracle ASM spreads files across all available storage. To protect against data loss, Oracle ASM extends the concept of SAME (stripe and mirror everything) and adds more flexibility as it can mirror at the database file level rather than at the entire disk level.

More importantly, Oracle ASM simplifies the processes of setting up mirroring, adding disks, and removing disks. Instead of managing hundreds or possibly thousands of files (as in a large data warehouse), DBAs using Oracle ASM create and administer a larger-grained object called a **disk group**. The disk group identifies the set of disks that are managed as a logical unit. Automation of file naming and placement of the underlying database files save administrators' time and ensure adherence to standard best practices.

The Oracle ASM native mirroring mechanism (two-way or three-way) protects against storage failures. With Oracle ASM mirroring, you can provide an additional level of data protection with the use of failure groups. A *failure group* is a set of disks sharing a common resource (disk controller or an entire disk array) whose failure can be tolerated. After it is defined, an Oracle ASM failure group intelligently places redundant copies of the data in separate failure groups. This ensures that the data is available and transparently protected against the failure of any component in the storage subsystem.

By using Oracle ASM, you can:

- ☐ Mirror and stripe across drives and storage arrays
- ☐ Automatically remirror from a failed drive to remaining drives
- ☐ Automatically rebalance stored data when disks are added or removed while the database remains online
- ☐ Support Oracle Database files and non-database files using Oracle Automatic Storage Management Cluster File System (Oracle ACFS)
- ☐ Allow for operational simplicity in managing database storage
- ☐ Manage the Oracle Cluster Registry (OCR) and voting disks
- ☐ Provide preferred read capability on disks that are local to the instance, which gives better performance for an extended cluster
- ☐ Support very large databases
- ☐ Support Oracle ASM rolling upgrades
- ☐ Support finer granularity in tuning and security
- ☐ Provide fast repair after a temporary disk failure through Oracle ASM Fast Mirror Resync and automatic repair of block corruptions if a good copy exists in one of the mirrors
- ☐ Provide disaster-recovery capability for the file system by enabling replication of Oracle ACFS across the network to a remote site.

Downloading Security Patches and Contacting Oracle Regarding Vulnerabilities:

Critical Patch Updates (CPU)

Critical Patch Updates (CPU) is a mechanism for preventing oracle security bug fix for its products. It will be released every Tuesday closets of every quarter in the month of Jan, Apr, Jul, and Oct. In addition, Oracle retains its ability to issue schedule patches or workaround instructions in case of particularly critical vulnerabilities when active exploits are reported globally. This is known as the Security Alert program, which is updated by Oracle in a frequent manner.

The following details will provide the benefits of CPU patches.

Maximum Security: The main idea behind this patch is to fill the hole in oracle products, which will lead customer data in vulnerability and its risk in terms of their business.

Lower Administrator Cost: A fixed CPU timetable removes the mystery from patch management. The calendar is additionally intended to keep away from the run of the outage dates during which clients cannot commonly change their production environment.

Simplified Patch Management: Patches are majorly cumulative. Therefore, they will eliminate all previously addressed vulnerability in Oracle Database.

Identification of architectural vulnerabilities: Security evaluations can be a key for architecture vulnerability identification.

The security updates for all products that receive CPUs are available to active Oracle Support customers on My Oracle Support. Follow the links below to learn more about Oracle's Security Fixing policies.

Oracle Security Vulnerability Disclosure Policies:

In order to prevent the risks to our customers, Oracle will not provide additional information about the specifics of vulnerabilities beyond what is provided in the CPU or Security Alert advisory and pre-release note, the pre-installation notes, the readme files, and FAQs. Oracle provides its customers with the same information in order to protect all customers equally. Oracle does not provide advance notification to individual customers.

How to Report Security Vulnerabilities to Oracle:

If you are a customer/partner, please use My Oracle Support to submit Service Request. If you are not, please do send an email to secalert_us@oracle.com.

GENERAL GUIDANCE FOR A BETTER INFRASTRUCTURE

Guidelines for securing Use Account and Privileges

1. Practice the principle of least privilege

> Grant necessary privileges only.
>
> Restrict library-related privileges to trusted users only.
>
> Restrict synonym-related privileges to trusted users only.
>
> Do not allow non-administrative users access to objects owned by the SYS schema.
>
> Restrict permissions on runtime facilities.

2. Lock and expire default (predefined) user accounts.

3. Use the following views to ensure that access is granted. Only users and roles that need access should be granted access to them.

```
DBA_*
DBA_ROLES
DBA_SYS_PRIVS
DBA_ROLE_PRIVS
DBA_TAB_PRIVS
DBA_AUDIT_TRAIL (if standard auditing is enabled)
DBA_FGA_AUDIT_TRAIL (if fine-grained auditing is enabled)
```

4. Monitor the granting of the following privileges only to users and roles that need these privileges.

> By default, Oracle Database audits the following privileges:

```
ALTER SYSTEM

AUDIT SYSTEM

CREATE EXTERNAL JOB
```

Oracle recommends that you also audit the following privileges:

```
ALL PRIVILEGES (which include privileges such as BECOME USER,
CREATE LIBRARY, and CREATE PROCEDURE)

DBMS_BACKUP_RESTORE package

EXECUTE to DBMS_SYS_SQL

SELECT ANY TABLE

SELECT on PERFSTAT.STATS$SQLTEXT

SELECT on PERFSTAT.STATS$SQL_SUMMARY

SELECT on SYS.SOURCE$

Privileges that have the WITH ADMIN clause

Privileges that have the WITH GRANT clause

Privileges that have the CREATE keyword
```

5. Revoke access to the following:

The SYS.USER_HISTORY$ table from all users except SYS and DBA accounts.

The RESOURCE role from typical application accounts.

The CONNECT role from typical application accounts.

The DBA role from users who do not need this role.

6. Grant privileges only to roles: Granting privileges to roles and not individual users makes the management and tracking of privileges much easier.

7. Limit the proxy account (for proxy authorization) privileges to CREATE SESSION only.

8. Use secure application roles to protect roles that are enabled by application code.

Guidelines for Securing Roles

1. Grant a role to users only if they need all privileges of the role.
2. Do not grant user roles to application developers.
3. Create and assign roles specific to each Oracle Database installation.
4. For enterprise users, create global roles.

Guidelines for Securing Passwords

1. Choose passwords carefully.
2. Create a longer, more complex password from a shorter, easier to remember password.
3. Ensure that the password is sufficiently complex.
4. Change default user passwords.
5. Change default passwords of administrative users.
6. Enforce password management.
7. Do not store user passwords in clear text in Oracle tables.

Guidelines for Securing Data

1. Enable data dictionary protection.
2. Restrict operating system access.
3. Encrypt sensitive data and all backup media that contains database files.

Guidelines for Securing a Database Installation and Configuration

1. Before you begin an Oracle Database installation on UNIX systems, ensure that the umask value is 022 for the Oracle owner account.
2. Install only what is required.
3. During installation, when you are prompted for a password, create a secure password.
4. Immediately after installation, lock and expire default user accounts.

Guidelines for Securing the Network

Network security can be improved by using client, listener, and network guidelines to ensure protection. Using SSL is an essential element in these lists, enabling top security for authentication and communications.

These guidelines include

securing the Client Connection,

securing the Network Connection, and

securing an SSL Connection.

Securing the Client Connection

1. Enforce access controls effectively and authenticate clients stringently.
2. Configure the connection to use encryption.
3. Set up strong authentication.

Securing the Network Connection

1. Use SSL when administering the listener.
2. Monitor listener activity.
3. Prevent online administration by requiring the administrator to have the write privilege on the listener password and on the listener.ora file on the server.
4. Do not set the listener password.
5. When a host computer has multiple IP addresses associated with multiple network interface controller (NIC) cards, configure the listener to the specific IP address.
6. Restrict the privileges of the listener, so that files cannot be read or written in the database or the Oracle server address space.
7. Use encryption to secure the data in-flight.
8. Use a firewall.
9. Prevent unauthorised administration of the Oracle listener.
10. Check network IP addresses.
11. Encrypt network traffic.

12. Secure the host operating system (the system on which Oracle Database is installed).

Securing an SSL Connection

1. Ensure that configuration files (for example, for clients and listeners) use the correct port for SSL, which is the port configured upon installation.

2. Ensure that TCPS is specified as the PROTOCOL in the ADDRESS parameter in the tnsnames.ora file (typically on the client or in the LDAP directory).

3. Ensure that the SSL mode is consistent for both ends of every communication. For example, the database (on one side) and the user or application (on the other) must have the same SSL mode.

4. Ensure that the server supports the client cipher suites and the certificate key algorithm in use.

5. Enable DN matching for both the server and client, to prevent the server from falsifying its identity to the client during connections.

6. Do not remove the encryption from your RSA private key inside your server.key file, which requires that you enter your pass phrase to read and parse this file.

REFERENCE

- Security Oracle Database 12c: A Technical Primer (Oracle Press)
- Securing the Oracle Database A Technical Primer (Oracle Press)
- https://ieeexplore.ieee.org/document/5386928
- https://docs.oracle.com/database/121/ADMQS/GUID-289A4BF6-F703-4ED5-8357- 89F651A6D1DE.htm#ADMQS12001
- https://docs.oracle.com/database/121/DVADM/dvintro.htm#DVADM70117
- https://docs.oracle.com/cd/E29597_01/server.1111/e17157/architectures.htm
- https://www.oracle.com/technetwork/database/availability/corruption-bestpractices-12c-2141348.pdf
- https://www.oracle.com/database/technologies/high-availability/oracle-database-maa-best-practices.html

- https://docs.oracle.com/cd/B28359_01/network.111/b28531/guidelines.htm#DBSEG009
- https://docs.oracle.com/cd/B28359_01/network.111/b28531/auditing.htm#DBSEG006
- https://www.oracle.com/emea/corporate/security-practices/assurance/vulnerability/disclosure.html
- Oracle® Database Security Guide- 11g Release 1 (11.1) B28531-21

SECURITY OF DATA ON THE CLOUD

DO WE REALLY NEED A CLOUD-BASED WEB APPLICATION FIREWALL FOR APPLICATIONS ON THE CLOUD?

Applications on the cloud are heavily prone to cyber-attacks such as SQL injection, cross-site scripting, brute force attacks, and DDoS attacks just to name a few. Businesses have their critical data on the cloud and the cloud service providers invest billions of dollars trying to secure the data on the cloud. The traditional security equipment do not suffice for securing the data, and there is a dire need to secure the application as the hackers and the malicious softwares attack the application directly. The solution to the problem is the implementation of a Web Application Firewall (WAF). The list of vulnerabilities and the threat to internet-facing applications has always been on the rise. Hackers have always been trying to crash the websites, intrude on to the application and steal the data. The intruders go to the extent of injecting a virus into the IT infrastructure. A powerful WAF can be very instrumental in blocking harmful incoming traffic.

It is also worthy to note that the market for WAF is changing drastically. While many enterprises are still relying on application-based WAF solutions, the cloud service providers are inclined toward a security platform approach that has an edge and is a combination of protection levels suited for distributed cloud environments such as private, public and hybrid clouds.

Having understood what exactly a WAF is, now let us understand in detail the need for it on the cloud:

1. WAF solution on the cloud scales up along with the business

The biggest advantage of using a cloud-based WAF is that it scales up to the need and is alert as a security guard all the time. A WAF on the cloud is normally configured as a reverse proxy and it is the initial entry point so to say it is the last line of defence before the incoming web traffic hits the internal applications tier.

If you have a WAF installed on your own, it may be a single point of failure unlike in the case of cloud-based WAFs. A key pro of using the cloud-based WAF is that it leverages the power of networks with geographically distributed points of presence. If the incoming web traffic is drastically on the rise, there is no need to worry as the cloud-based WAF will rise to the occasion, make use of the underlying cloud infrastructure, and immediately isolate the endpoints from the incoming threats.

2. WAF solution on the cloud handles the threat much before it reaches the cloud infrastructure

As the saying goes in the English language, "Prevention is better than cure", so the cloud-based WAF solution blocks the malicious traffic much before it reaches the cloud infrastructure network. It is always better if the bad traffic is identified further away and it is turned away before it reaches the application on the cloud infrastructure. Therefore, it is very clear that the cloud-based WAFs keep the perimeter of the cloud infrastructure very safe to a very larger extent. This security perimeter factor gives the cloud-based WAF solution an edge over the normal firewalls.

3. WAF solution on the cloud ensures enhanced security for multicloud implementations

The current day technology and the business demand that there has to be a combination of different cloud environments in an enterprise. Most of the organizations today adopt the policy of adopting multi-cloud environments and the concept of a hybrid cloud. The best cloud-based WAFs support the web applications on public, private, hybrid clouds and the on-premise web applications. Therefore, it is very important to choose the right WAF on the cloud, as the right cloud-based WAF provides an independent platform that helps in securing all internet-facing applications irrespective of whether they reside on the cloud or on-premise.

4. WAF is managed by the CSP. That really makes it easy for the customer! Isn't it?

The best of cloud service providers have a team of their own who are experts in security and they manage the complete WAF for the customers on their cloud infrastructure. There is a significant reduction in the risk to the internet-facing applications when the WAF is managed by the cloud service provider as security is a big challenge and one of the critical criteria on the cloud.

The monitoring, tuning, upgradation and complete maintenance of the WAF hardware are managed by the cloud vendor, which reduces a big burden for the customer. The high commitment and delivery standards given by the cloud vendor protects the business from sudden downtimes and saves the customers brand. Furthermore, the managed services give the customer an edge by helping them spend their time on managing their core business.

5. Zero CAPEX and very minimal OPEX

It is very clearly understood that with the WAF on the cloud, you do not have to invest in the hardware. The CAPEX costs are borne by the cloud service provider. The cloud vendor gives different subscription pricing and the customer has the luxury of choosing among the various options based on the usage and the need. The customer can choose the "PAY AS YOU GO" model and, at the same time, enjoy the benefits by keeping the applications secure from the malicious traffic. These flexible payment models make it easier for the customer to plan their annual budget.

TOP TEN POINTS TO BEAR IN MIND BEFORE FINALIZING A CLOUD-BASED WAF

The threat landscape is expanding enormously, so there is a dire need that the security providers also strengthen their products such as the WAFs. Over the years, there has been tremendous growth in the list of WAF providers as there are many new startups as well. Bearing these factors in mind, it is very much essential that organizations analyse and understand the existing Web Applications in detail and then decide as to which one has to be chosen for their enterprise. WAFs need to have the capability of discerning malicious and fraudulent traffic from legitimate traffic. It is a very challenging and demanding task for any security professional as hackers today try to weave their fraudulent content within safe looking incoming traffic.

Just check whether the below set of questions get an answer "YES". If the answer is "YES", then you may consider choosing a particular cloud-based WAF.

1. Can this WAF protect the applications from the malicious threats across the entire hybrid cloud of enterprise and the multi-cloud environment as well? It should be one single solution that can support the whole enterprise irrespective of the application of the infrastructure behind it.

....

2. Is the solution a complete cloud-based WAF and not just a stand-alone Web Application Firewall or a web application firewall that has been installed on top of a virtual machine (VM) on the cloud?

   ....

3. Is the WAF on this cloud a stable one and does not have a single point of failure and has a global presence?

   ....

4. Is the team that manages this WAF solution on the cloud a certified team in the area of security and are they experts in Firewalls on the cloud?

   ....

5. Does this cloud service provider give you support 24×7 in case of any issues?

   ....

6. Will this cloud WAF solution isolate the applications and the underlying infrastructure from cyber threats and at the same ensure that the applications behind the WAF cloud get the traffic only from the WAF and not directly?

   ....

7. Will the cloud-based WAF provider support you in the future as well, when there is an enhancement of your business and more application servers are added?

   ....

8. Are the costs reasonable for the services offered and are they acceptable as per market standards?

   ....

9. At the time of patching or upgradation of the WAF, does your cloud vendor assign a designated resource for your organization?

   ....

10. Is there a special plan given by your cloud vendor to manage the "Distributed Denial-of-Service" Layer 7 DDoS attack?

....

TOP SECURITY POLICIES TO SECURE AZURE

Gone are those days, enterprises depended on custom, in-house created applications facilitated in their own datacentres. Having perceived the benefits of cloud computing, throughout the most recent five years these applications have gradually moved to public, private, or hybrid cloud. Cloud use has arrived at a tipping point, and setup of test and production application systems on the cloud has been on the significant rise at the expense of on-premise datacentres. It is observed across the industry that organizations are progressively developing and deploying new custom applications on Infrastructure as a service (IaaS) platforms like Microsoft Azure, however enterprises are also performing lift and shift for their current custom applications from on-premise to the cloud.

While well-known out-of-the-box SaaS items like Salesforce, Box, Dropbox, and Office 365 are getting to be normal in the work environment, still enterprises have business needs that require specially designed custom applications. Therefore, even if these SAAS applications are secured by the cloud service providers, it is a huge responsibility on the part of the customer to share the responsibility of securing custom applications.

Security Challenges with Azure

Businesses cannot bear to have their Azure cloud or on the other hand the custom applications running on Azure, compromised. Organizations store sensitive and critical information, for example, credit card numbers and Social Security numbers are stored in custom applications. Furthermore, it is observed that more than 60-70% of the enterprises have business-critical applications that cannot afford downtime, if it encountered an unplanned or an emergency downtime it would incredibly affect the IT team's capacity to work and deliver the service to the business. For instance, a bank cannot function if the ATM machines or its critical databases are down. An airline cannot function if its flight path application is not working, as the pilots cannot navigate the aircraft.

Threats to applications and databases running on Microsoft Azure cloud and the information within them can take numerous structures:

Denial-of-Service (DoS) Attack on an Application

Microsoft Azure has created modern DoS assurance abilities as mentioned in the Azure Marketplace. Nevertheless, it is possible that an enormous assault could overpower Azure's safeguards and take an application running on the Azure cloud disconnected for a while until the assault is remediated.

Threats Because of Users With Privilege

It is observed that more than half of the enterprises encounter 10.9 insider dangers what's more, 3.3 privilege user threats every month. These occurrences incorporate both malignant and careless conduct. As a rule, good-natured representatives will misconfigure an Azure administration or something else ignore a basic security control that will uncover the venture to security dangers, yet dangers can emerge out of privileged or malicious users too.

Third-party Account Compromise

As per the Verizon Data Breach Investigations Report, 63% of data breaches were because of an account that was compromised where the individual hacking was made use of a weak, default, or stolen secret key. Misconfigured security settings or user IDs that have an unnecessary identity and access management (IAM) privileges can increase the potential harm.

Sensitive Information Transferred to Cloud Against Strategy/Guideline

Numerous Enterprises have industry-explicit regional guidelines or internal policies that deny certain kinds of information from being transferred to the cloud. In a few cases, information can be securely put in the cloud, however, just in certain geographic areas (for example datacentre in UAE, however, not in the USA).

Security Factors Are Not Considered in Software Development

There should be a stringent practice that checks for threats from all angles when the software is developed. However, currently most of the organizations give importance to the quality of software at the time of delivery, rather emphasis should be strictly made so that even security factor is dealt at the ground level with high importance.

1. 'Data collection' should be set to on.

   Automatic provisioning of monitoring agent has to be enabled for gathering security information. At the point when automatic provisioning of monitoring agent is turned on, Azure Security Centre provisions the Microsoft Monitoring Agent on all existing upheld Azure VMs as well as the ones that have been created. The Microsoft Monitoring agent gives cautions and checks for any security-related configurations and events, for example, updates to the system, OS vulnerabilities, and endpoint protection.

2. 'System updates' should be set to on.

   Ensure system updates recommendations are enabled for VMs. At the point when this setting has been done, Azure Security Centre recovers a day by day rundown of available security and important updates from Windows Update or on the other hand Windows Server Update Services. The list that is given by the system rundown relies upon the administration that is arranged for that VM and prescribes that the missing updates be applied on to the system. With regards to Linux systems, the strategy utilises the distro-given package management system to determine packages that have the latest updates, which can be applied. It likewise checks for security and important system updates from Azure VMs.

3. 'OS vulnerabilities' should be set to on.

   OS vulnerabilities recommendations have to be enabled for VMs, so that it could give the suggestions to be incorporated. At the point when this setting is empowered, it investigates operating system configurations on a day-to-day basis to find out issues that could make the VMs helpless against assault. The policies moreover suggest configuration changes to address these vulnerabilities.

4. 'Endpoint protection' should be set to on.

   Ensure endpoint security suggestions for VMs are enabled. At the point when this setting is enabled, Azure Security Centre suggests endpoint protection be provisioned for all Windows VMs to help recognise and expel infections, spyware, and different vindictive programming.

5. 'Disk encryption' should be set to on.

   Ensure the disk encryption feature is enabled so that it can give suggestions for VMs. At the point when this setting is done, Azure Security Centre suggests enabling disk encryption in every VM to improve information security to a larger extent.

6. 'Network security groups' should be set to on.

   It is very significant that network security groups' recommendations are enabled for VMs. At the point when this setting has been setup, Azure Security Centre suggests that network security groups be setup to control inbound and outbound traffic to VMs that have open endpoints. Network security groups that are setup for a subnet is acquired by all VM network interfaces except if something else has been mentioned. Apart from evaluating that a network security group is configured, this policy once setup also evalutates the inbound security rules so that it can curb and control the malicious incoming traffic.

7. 'WAF' should be set to on.

Ensure WAF suggestions are enabled for VMs. At the point when this setting has been setup, Azure Security Centre suggests that a WAF be provisioned on VMs when any of the below options are true:

   a. Instance-level open IP is utilised and the inbound security rules for the related system security gathering are setup to enable access to port 80/443.
   b. Load-balanced IP is utilised and the related load balancing for workloads and inbound network address translation (NAT) rules are designed to permit access to port 80/443.

8. 'Next-generation firewall' should be set to on.
It enables the cutting edge firewall setups for VMs. At the point when this setting has been done, it broadens network protections beyond network security groups, which are incorporated with Azure. Azure Security Centre will find deployments for which a high-end next-generation firewall is suggested and it enables you to have a VM.

9. 'Vulnerability assessment' should be set to on.

Vulnerability assessment suggestions will be enabled with the setup of this policy for VMs. At the point when this setting is empowered, Azure Security Centre suggests a vulnerability assessment solution be installed on the VM.

10. 'Storage encryption' should be set to on.

This is an excellent feature. Once this setup has been done, it will give storage encryption recommendations. Once the suggested recommendations have been incorporated, it will help in the encryption of new data in Azure blobs and the files within it will be encrypted.

11. 'JIT network access' should be set to on.

JIT system access will be enabled for VMs with this policy. At the point when this setting is done, the Azure Security Centre secures inbound traffic to the Azure VMs by making an NSG rule. You select the ports on the VM to which inbound traffic ought to be bolted down. Just in time, VM access can be utilised to bolt down inbound traffic to your Azure VMs, lessening presentation to assaults while giving simple access to associate with VMs when required.

12. 'SQL encryption' should be set to on.

SQL encryption suggestions will be enabled. At the point when this setting is enabled, Azure Security Centre suggests that encryption very still be empowered for your Azure SQL Database, dependent backups, and transaction log files. Therefore, it goes to the extent that even if the data is breached, it will not be harmful as the stolen content will not be in a human-readable format.

WHAT'S ORACLE CASB?

Oracle Cloud Access Security Broker examines the security of Oracle Cloud Infrastructure setups through a blend of predefined, Oracle Cloud Infrastructure explicit security controls and methodologies, client configurable security controls and strategies and propelled security tests utilizing the concepts of Artificial Intelligence for figuring out malicious content. Oracle CASB security also assists with checking and identifying the wrongly configured Oracle Cloud Infrastructure resources, observing credentials and the privileges provided, the study of user behavioural patterns and data gathering using machine learning for identification of events related to risks.

Oracle Cloud Access Security Broker is an excellent option for monitoring the Oracle Cloud Infrastructure. An Oracle Cloud Infrastructure application has to be created with Oracle CASB and provisioned with the API key credentials of a user ID that has the minimum privileges of IAM user and should have access to get some basic information such as details of the configuration and audit logs from the tenancy of Oracle Cloud Infrastructure.

Oracle CASB intermittently gathers the configuration details of the tenancy along with the audit logs for the security investigation and sends alerts to the concerned stakeholders for any deviations from the security standards.

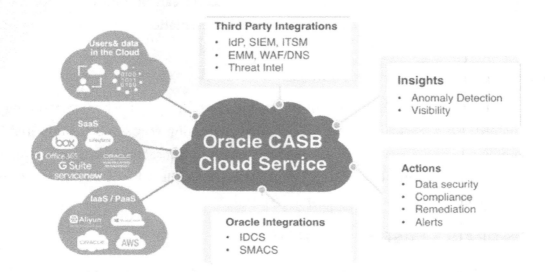

In spite of the fact that cloud service providers incorporate security for their hardware, it is the responsibility of the customer as well to secure access to the information and applications in the cloud.

A Cloud Access Security Broker (CASB) works on the principle of certain key functions:

Visibility

While checking your cloud applications, you see all action in light of user, network, database, application or device. Oracle CASB Cloud Service gives a view into various kinds of dangers related to clients of the cloud applications, for example,

- User behaviour, which is dependent on deviations from typical use history

- Suspicious movement, for example, a client interchanging between geographic areas
- Noncompliant security control, for example, a password that is not really complex and strong
- Policy alerts dependent on certain rules and regulations, about who gets to what application databases or servers, how they get to them, and from where

Compliance

Oracle CASB Cloud Service accompanies predefined security controls. These controls guarantee that your cloud applications are checked to a high level of security. For instance, it enables you to determine security control benchmark settings for an application and afterwards alarms you to take any action that does not agree to those settings.

To guarantee and record consistency with approaches and guidelines, Oracle CASB Cloud Service gives reports about different sorts of exercises for your cloud applications. You can produce reports, for example, the rotation status of the keys used to get to Amazon Web Services (AWS).

Data Security

Delicate and sensitive data requires progressively stringent controls. The controls are designed with policies that trigger alerts.

For instance, a strategy can be setup that alarms when an email is sent on the off chance that it meets determined conditions, for example, a suspicious IP address, domain destination, or a timestamp after the working hours. At that point, if an Office365 cloud application client sends an exchange email to a noncorporate beneficiary, a risk is highlighted.

You can likewise setup a strategy that creates alerts dependent on unsafe administrator activities, for example, changing the rules that have been setup in place by the exchange server before the email is sent.

Threat Protection

Oracle CASB Cloud Service gives a high level of transparency into the activities that take place in the applications on the cloud. Threat discovery happens when the action for your cloud applications is outside the typical limits. For example, let us see some suspicious happenings:

- Excessive non-successful attempts from an IP address
- Different client behavioural patterns based on history
- Policy alert warning created from a strategy infringement

Easy Monitoring

1. Accumulate data safely

Set up a dedicated service user in the cloud application to give Oracle CASB Cloud Service secure access to data, for example, logs, required for checking.

2. Keep a close eye on the cloud platforms

Utilise the adaptability of the Oracle CASB Cloud Service predefined layouts not exclusively to screen your cloud stages, yet additionally to bolster various degrees of checking (Checking Only, for all supported cloud administrations, or Push Security Controls, for AWS, Box, or on the other hand Salesforce).

3. Set security controls.

Setup a degree of control that is more secure than the cloud-stage defaults. With the improved observation and implementation of your security strategy, you can verify your cloud and guarantee that it remains secure.

Response to the Incidents

Oracle CASB Cloud Service figures out on its own and creates incidents in light of distinguished dangers and observed threats. They can be remediated in one of the below-mentioned ways:

- Manual: An administrator fixes the issue.

- Automatic: For certain types of incidents, Oracle CASB Cloud Service based on its functionality of remediation framework consequently fixes the issue in the cloud infrastructure; for instance, making a password policy even stronger.
- Delegation: It includes the gathering of incidents and sending out the occurrences to a unified and centralised ticketing application, for example, ServiceNow.

Analytics for User Behaviour

Oracle CASB Cloud Service uses machine-learning capacities to assign risk scores based on the activity of the client. Current client activity is contrasted with the baseline activity to recognise the behaviour that is not normal. An incident is recorded and can incorporate an alternative for the administrator to automatically remediate, such as blocking an IP address and resetting a client's password. Client practices that can cause a high-hazard score incorporate exercises that are outside the ordinary conduct for a kind of movement, for example, the number of downloads, logins, or failed logins. In fact, even the activity of the administrators is likewise investigated, because the potential risk is more noteworthy. A client who jumps between multiple geographical locations is also a marker of risk.

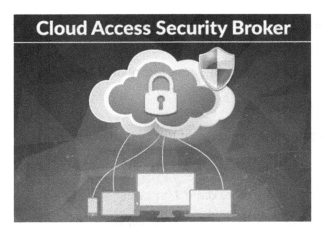

In conclusion, we can understand that Oracle CASB plays a very significant role in the concept of security on the cloud. It assists the enterprises to enjoy the full benefits of the cloud and at the same time have their data secured. Oracle's CASB supports IaaS, PaaS and

SaaS. For example, Oracle CASB also supports the offerings in IaaS from other cloud vendors such as AWS, Microsoft Azure and Rackspace. The Saas offerings such as ServiceNow, Box, Microsoft Office 365, Google Apps, GitHub and Salesforce are also supported by Oracle CASB.

PROTECT YOUR DATA WITH ORACLE DATA SAFE

Data is one of any organizations significant resources. In the event that this data is not protected appropriately, this data can turn into the greatest liability for the organization. Simply get the feedback from the organizations who have been in the news after they encountered a huge data breach due to vulnerable attacks, they would confirm that they not only lost confidential data, IP information, but also often got a bad name for their brand and also brought about huge remediation costs and fines.

With the present hackers in the digital era, utilizing progressed, automated hacking devices, regular businesses with restricted skillsets in the field of security, time, or tools that do not stand an opportunity against this awry fighting. The question does not remain as to whether the businesses who are not prepared will be breached or not, rather when will they get breached? Without innovation and technology, most enterprises are easy targets and hackers love to target such organizations first. We have to reevaluate how to shield databases, the vault of most delicate information related to the business.

Concerns from the Customers

As we take a deep dive into the concerns of the customers, the below concerns pocket up:

Are my databases setup safely? Are there any loopholes in it?

Where is the critical sensitive data? Is it safe?

Who are those potential risky users whom the database administrator needs to be aware of? What is the nature of their job role? What might they do, if they are given the privileges?

What are those compliance requirements? Can it be met?

What about Cloud? When my data is on the cloud, will it be safe as my on-premise?

In the concept of tenancy on the public cloud, how will my data be secure?

The customers always want their applications to be secure 24×7×365, because any attack could prompt an absolute misfortune. In any case, securing is not straight and an easy task without proper automation and unification.

Features of Oracle Data Safe

In light of addressing client concerns with regards to security, Oracle has developed Oracle Data Safe – a cutting edge, brought together, and automated security service concept to help safeguard clients' databases on Oracle Cloud. Data Safe is intended to distinguish gaps in their cautious stance, give clarity into security issues with information, users, applications, and give suggestions on the best way to contain security risks.

Oracle has clubbed five significant capabilities, which make Oracle Data Safe as a key and an unparalleled product concerning security.

Security Assessment

Poor database setups, for example, feeble password strategies, no controls on over-privileged records, and absence of activity monitoring are the most widely recognised reasons for vulnerabilities in Cloud databases.

In Oracle Data Safe, Security Assessment examines your database designs, user access and security controls, and after that reports discoveries with suggestions for remediation exercises that pursue best practices to decrease or alleviate hazard.

The Security Assessment reports give the reader a general image of the database security status. They feature proposals by the following certified bodies, making it simpler for the reader to recognise the suggested security controls:

Centre for Internet Security (CIS),

European Union's General Data Protection Regulation (GDPR), and

Security Technical Implementation Guide (STIG).

It classifies and organises these risks with the goal that you can choose which ones to address first.

Instances of what you may do with the Security Assessment highlight

- ☐ Quickly and effectively survey your database setups to realise which arrangement decisions may have brought superfluous hazard into your condition and how you can lessen, evacuate, or alleviate dangers.
- ☐ Apply security discoveries to ensure compliance with the European Union's GDPR and different guidelines.
- ☐ Identify the security strategies that are already in place on the system.
- ☐ Guidance on how to secure sensitive information in your Cloud databases when moving applications from lower environments to production. Security Assessment may recommend that the encryption be done and after that, it will guide you with the methodologies on the most proficient method to do that.
- ☐ Promote database security best methodologies.

The Security Assessment enlightens with the below-mentioned reports, which help in the security of the data:

☐ Comprehensive Assessments
☐ Security Controls
☐ User Security
☐ Security Configurations

Data Discovery

Data Discovery plays a very crucial role in finding sensitive data in the Oracle Cloud databases.

Securing sensitive information starts with realising what delicate information exists in the database, and where it is found. Data Discovery investigates the metadata and actual information in the Oracle Cloud databases to find sensitive information and gives extensive outcomes highlighting the sensitive columns and related data.

Data Discovery utilises sensitive types that characterise the sorts of information to search for. Oracle Data Safe gives more than 125 predefined sensitive types that you can use to look through sensitive information. The sensitive types include individual information relating to distinguishing proof, biographic, IT, financial, social insurance, work, and scholarly data. You can likewise make your very own sensitive types. The predefined sensitive types are segregated under classifications, making it simple to discover and utilise relevant sensitive types. You reveal to Data Discovery what to search for, and it finds those specific sensitive columns that meet the mentioned criteria.

You can alternatively gather test information from your objective databases. Test information can enable you to approve the found delicate sections. You ought to be cautious while utilizing this component, in any case, as it gathers touchy information. Just approved individuals ought to have the option to gather and see the sample information.

Data Discovery saves the results captured as a sensitive data model (SDM). An SDM comprises of found sensitive columns and referential connections. You can perform incremental updates to an SDM and physically include and expel columns from an SDM.

You can utilise an SDM to actualise other security controls, for example, data masking. For instance, you can characterise a masking policy utilizing an SDM and use it to mask the sensitive information on the specific databases.

SDMs get put away in the Oracle Data Safe Library, empowering you to reuse an SDM for numerous masking policies. SDMs can be exported and imported into other Oracle Data Safe Libraries so that they can be used again. The confirmation highlight distinguishes any contrasts between an SDM and a specific target database.

To enable you to comprehend the sensitive information and for record-keeping, Data Discovery gives a report that rundowns the delicate sections and insights regarding those segments. The sensitive columns are sorted dependent on their sensitive types. The report likewise incorporates the complete number of critical tables, columns, and information found. A chart gives you a chance to analyse the measure of sensitive information at sensitive classification class and sensitive type levels. You can likewise download this report from the Oracle Data Safe console.

Sensitive types are classified into sensitive classifications. When you make your own sensitive types, you segregate into different sensitive categories for them. The top-level classifications for predefined categories are as per the following:

Sensitive Type	Examples
Identification Information	US Social Security Number (SSN), Visa Number, and Full Name
Biographic Information	Date of Birth, Full Address, Mother's Maiden Name, Religion
IT Information	Password, User ID, Hostname, IP Address
Financial Information	CVV Number PIN, Credit Card Number, Bank Account Number, Login and password for Bank account
Healthcare Information	Health Insurance Number, Healthcare Provider Name, Blood Group
Employment Information	Joining Date, Separation Date, Job Title, Salary, Employee ID
Academic Information	College Name, Financial Support, Grade

Data Masking

The Data Masking concept of Oracle Data Safe helps in concealing sensitive information in non-production databases.

Oracle Data Safe gives a thorough setup of formats for masking data to enable you to veil regular sensitive and individual information, for example, names, national identifiers, credit card information, telephone numbers, and religion.

Furthermore, additional masking choices are there, for example, rearranging, encryption, and replacing with some other numbers, strings, and dates. Oracle Data Safe gives you the ability to effectively make new masking formats, without requiring any specialised skillset. You can store these user-defined masking formats in Oracle Data Safe Library so that it can be used later based on the requirement.

Thus, you can make masking policies and store them in the Oracle Data Safe Library. You can utilise this feature and the masking approach to veil distinctive target databases. The masking policy can also be downloaded as an XML document, altered and transferred to the equivalent or an alternate Oracle Data Safe Library.

Data Masking creates a concealing report that recapitulates the data that was masked in the database. For instance, the report reveals to you the names of the sensitive columns veiled, the different masking formats utilised, and the final number of tables and the data concealed.

The Data Masking section of Oracle Data Safe plays a very crucial role in the masking area.

It improves the way toward concealing confidential information in the non-production databases by giving an automated, adaptable, and an easy setup. It gives the capability of doing the following:

- Maximise the business usage of the information without uncovering the critical information
- Masking of Oracle databases facilitated on Oracle Cloud
- Use different masking strategies to meet the particular business necessities

☐ Preserve information uprightness guaranteeing that the covered information keeps on working with applications

User Assessment

The key requirement to manage sensitive data is to first identify the list of users who have access to this critical information. The accounts that have powerful privileges should be figured out, for example, Database Administrator, Audit Administrator or Database Vault Administrator. Who can have changes done that can affect the complete system, get to delicate information, or award access to unapproved clients? Is there a danger of ethical hackers assuming control over some client accounts in light of the fact that the passwords have not been changed in quite a while?

The User Assessment includes in Oracle Data Safe answers these inquiries and more to enable you to distinguish your risky users. The database administrators would then be able to identify suitable areas of risk and accordingly deploy security controls and approaches.

User Assessment surveys data about the users in the data dictionaries in the database that you have chosen for examination, and afterwards computes a hazard score for every user. For instance, it assesses the user types, how the user authentication process is done, the password policies doled out to every user, and for the duration since the particular user had changed the password. With this data, you can choose whether to do the implementation of stringent password policies, use Oracle Database Vault, or plan out a different approach to further limit client access.

Activity Auditing

Oracle Data Safe can follow database user activity and raise alarms on dangerous activities, an absolute necessity based on a few policies and regulations of the organization. You can choose from default audit policies for normal and privileged accounts and utilise one of the numerous out-of-the-case audit reports for different database exercises. You can hold the audit information for as long as a year for investigation on the off chance that something were to turn out badly.

With Activity Auditing, you can screen user activities on Oracle Cloud databases, gather and hold review records per industry and administrative compliance requirements and trigger alarms as required for unordinary or doubtful behavioural patterns. You can review sensitive database changes, administrator and user activities, activities prescribed by the CIS, and activities characterised by your very own Information technology and audit departments. You can be cautioned when a database parameter or review arrangement changes, a fizzled login by an administrator happens, a user account privilege changes, and when a user account is created or removed.

SECURING EMAIL DELIVERY IN OCI

Despite the fact that email security has unquestionably improved since its initiation, (for example, the usage of encrypted passwords), it is a long way from being a totally secure method for transmitting significant data. For instance, an email does not just go from the sender to the beneficiary promptly.

Today, there are four fundamental spots where the vast majority's email can be undermined:

- On the server(s)
- On the cloud
- Over the networks
- On the email recipients device

The Email Delivery capability within Oracle Cloud Infrastructure offers an SMTP (Simple Mail Transfer Protocol) endpoint, secured with the help of a password that is generated in the console. The SMTP password is essential for sending messages utilizing Email Delivery. Oracle suggests that you make a different IAM user account for SMTP. This user must be privileged with manage permissions for approved-senders and suppressions resource types. Oracle strongly suggests that the SMTP credentials are stored safely and intermittently changed.

Generation of SMTP Credentials for a User Account

SMTP credentials are required for sending email through Email Delivery. Every user account is constrained to a limit of two SMTP credentials. On the off chance that more than two are required, SMTP credentials must be produced on other existing user accounts or more user accounts must be made.

1. Click on Create user as shown in the below snapshot, so that this user account can be used for securing email delivery.

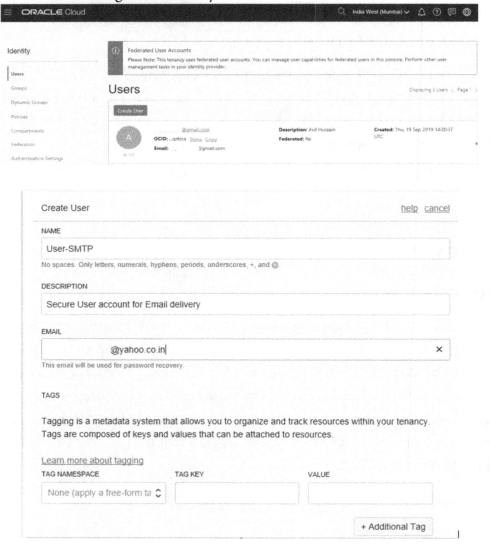

Create

2. Follow the navigation menu. Go to the tab "Governance and Administration", go to Identity and click Users.

Find out the user in the list that has the required privileges to manage email, and then ensure to click the user's name to view the information.

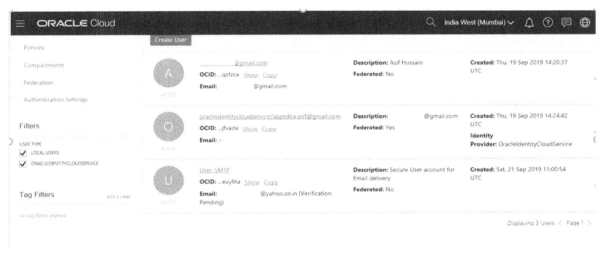

3. Click on SMTP Credentials.

4. Click Generate SMTP Credentials.

5. Enter a Description of the SMTP Credentials in the dialog box.

6. Click Generate SMTP Credentials to generate the credentials. A user name and password will be displayed.

7. Ensure to copy the user name and password for future use and click Close.

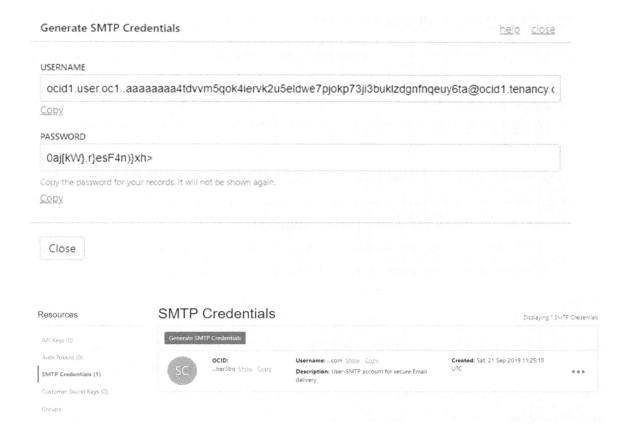

As per the security standpoint, it is always better to generate SMTP credentials for a newly created user account rather than the console user account that already has the required permissions to it.

ENCRYPTING BLOCK VOLUME IN OCI

Volumes are of two types such as block volumes and boot volumes. Block volumes are very beneficial as they help in instant storage capacity to be extended progressively. The compute instance can be booted using the boot volume. The IAM service bunches the group of related volume resource types into a joined resource type called volume-family.

It is a security recommendation to assign the least privileged access for IAM user accounts to resource types in volume-family. Volumes, volume-attachments and volume-backups are the resource types that comprise the volume-family. The volume-family resources can be detached and allow the dynamic extension of storage. They may also contain the required image for instance booting. The volume-attachments resources connect volumes and instances. The volume-backups resources are point-in-time duplicates of volumes that can be utilised to make block volumes or even recover block volumes if required.

To limit the loss of information because of accidental erases by an authorised user account or by malicious activity, Oracle suggests to giving VOLUME_DELETE, VOLUME_ATTACHMENT_DELETE and VOLUME_BACKUP_DELETE authorizations to a bare minimum list of IAM user accounts and groups. DELETE privilege ought to be offered distinctly to tenancy and compartment administrators. To limit the loss of information due to corruption or human error or deletions, Oracle suggests that you make backups of volumes on a periodical basis. Oracle Cloud Infrastructure permits automated backups, which can be scheduled.

Volumes and the corresponding backups are encrypted utilizing AES-256. You can likewise encode your data volumes utilizing options such as dm-crypt, veracrypt, and Bit-Locker.

The steps for encryption using dm-crypt are introduced in the following section.

dm-crypt is a kernel-level encryption methodology that gives volumes that are encrypted. It encodes information that resides on the filesystem (for instance, ext4 and NTFS), and the same is stored on a storage device in the Linux Unified Key Setup (LUKS) group. The Loopback devices assist in storing the encrypted volumes on the disk, disk partition, logical volume, or file-backed storage. Cryptsetup is the client level utility that takes care of dm-crypt and is used in the encryption of files and partitions. dm-crypt utilises the Linux crypto APIs for encryption activity. 'dm-crypt' can be used to encrypt non-root volumes:

'dm-crypt' can be used to encrypt non-root volumes:

1. Block storage volume should be attached to an instance (for example, /dev/sdb).
2. '/dev/sdb' should be formatted for LUKS encryption. Enter LUKS passphrase when prompted.

The passphrase is utilised to encrypt the LUKS master key, which is used for encrypting the volume.

```
cryptsetup -y luksFormat /dev/sdb
```

3. Ensure that the LUKS formatting is successful.

```
cryptsetup isLuks /dev/sdb && echo Success
```

4. Retreive encryption information about the device.

```
cryptsetup luksDump /dev/sdb
```

5. Retreive LUKS UUID of the device. The UUID value is useful in configuring the /etc/crypttab.

```
cryptsetup luksUUID /dev/sdb
```

6. A LUKS container has to be created with device name, dev_name. This also creates a device node, /dev/mapper/<dev_name>.

```
cryptsetup luksOpen /dev/sdb <dev_name>
```

7. Retrieve information for the mapped device.

```
dmsetup info <dev_name>
```

8. The device node has to be formatted as an ext4 filesystem.

```
sudo mkfs -t ext4 /dev/sdb
```

9. The device node has to be mounted.

```
mount /dev/mapper/<dev_name> /home/encrypt_fs
```

10. An entry has to be added in /etc/crypttab.

```
<dev_name> UUID=<LUKS UUID of /dev/sdb> none
```

All of the files copied to /home/encrypt_fs are encrypted by LUKS.

11. The keyfile has to be added to an available keyslot of the encrypted volume. This keyfile is helpful in accessing the encrypted volume.

```
dd if=/dev/urandom of=$HOME/keyfile bs=32 count=1

chmod 600 $HOME/keyfile

cryptsetup luksAddKey /dev/sdb ~/keyfile
```

12. Check the encryption status of files.

```
cryptsetup status /home/encrypt_fs
```

13. Unmount once done.

```
umount /home/encrypt_fs

cryptsetup luksClose <dev_name>
```

The Data Volumes that were encrypted using 'dm-crypt' can be remotely mounted as detailed below:

The steps mentioned below are based on the fact that the keyfile is on an on-premises host (SRC_IP) and that <OCI_SSH_KEY> is the SSH private key of the instance.

1. The keyfile has to be copied from the on-premises host to an instance.

```
scp -i <OCI_SSH_KEY> keyfile opc@SRC_IP:/home/opc
```

2. The encrypted volume has to be opened.

```
ssh i <OCI_SSH_KEY> opc@SRC_IP "cryptsetup luksOpen /dev/sdb
<dev_name> --key-file=/home/opc/keyfile"
```

3. The below syntax has to be used for mounting the volume.

```
ssh -i <OCI_SSH_KEY> opc@SRC_IP "mount /dev/mapper/<dev_name>
/home/encrypt_fs"
```

4. Operations can be done on the data in the mounted volume.

5. The encrypted volume has to be unmounted as below.

```
ssh -i <OCI_SSH_KEY> opc@SRC_IP "umount /home/encrypt_fs"

ssh -i <OCI_SSH_KEY> opc@SRC_IP "cryptsetup luksClose
<dev_name>"
```

6. The keyfile has to be deleted from the instance as shown below.

```
ssh -i <OCI_SSH_KEY> opc@SRC_IP "\rm -f /home/opc/keyfile"
```

It is fitting to conclude that Oracle uses the concept of 'dm-crypt' encryption to secure the data stored in block volumes in Oracle Cloud Infrastructure.

HIGH AVAILABILITY FOR DATABASE ON OCI

The Oracle Cloud Infrastructure Database administration lets you rapidly start an Oracle Database System and make at least one database on it. This Database service bolsters a few kinds of DB Systems, of different sizes, cost, and performance.

DB Systems With Exadata Capability

Exadata DB Systems enable you to use the intensity of Exadata inside the Oracle Cloud Infrastructure. Furthermore, the best part is that an Exadata DB System comprises of a quarter rack, half rack, full rack of Compute nodes and the storage servers, integrated by a high performing, very low-latency InfiniBand network and of course the main Exadata software.

The automatic backups can be configured, optimised to accommodate workloads of different levels, and scale up the complete system to satisfy expanded needs. Exadata DB systems on Oracle Cloud Infrastructure gives the full benefits as the on-premises Exadata DB system. It is one system that has the best of breed components with very high capability that can suit any kind of high-end business with large volumes of processing, storage and loads.

DB Systems with RAC capability

Oracle Cloud Infrastructure makes the databases highly available with 2-node RAC DB Systems on VM Compute instances. Oracle strongly recommends using 2-node RAC database systems offering on the cloud as that helps in keeping the systems available online if the primary node goes down. The database service can also be configured to back up the database to Oracle Cloud Infrastructure Object Storage.

The diagram shown below gives a glimpse as to how a 2-node RAC DB System can keep the systems online:

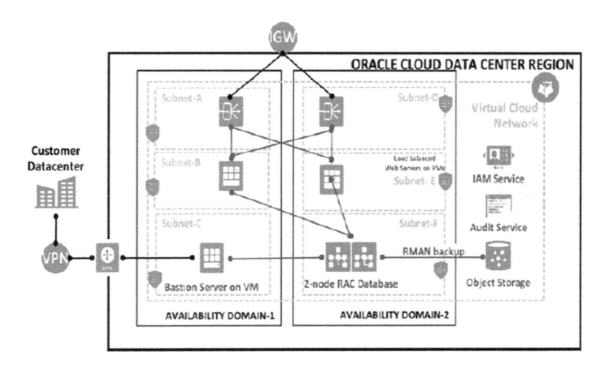

Data Guard Capability on DB Systems

Oracle Data Guard guarantees high accessibility, information assurance, and the capability of disaster recovery for business data. Data Guard gives a high sense of comfort to the customers with its extensive list of capabilities that assist the Database Administrators in creation, maintenance, management and monitoring of standby databases to empower production Oracle databases to endure disasters and corruptions of the information within the database. Data Guard keeps up these standby databases as duplicates of the production database. At any point, if the production database goes down in view of a planned or an unforeseen blackout, Data Guard can switch any standby database to the production database, limiting the time related with the blackout.

Usage of Data Guard in the Oracle Cloud Infrastructure requires two databases, the first database of course in a primary role and the other in a standby role. The two databases make a Data Guard affiliation. The applications that connect to these databases connect to the primary database, which is the production database. The standby database is a value-based steady duplicate of the production database.

It is recommended by Oracle in their best practices that DB system of the production database should be kept in a different availability domain than the DB System of the standby database. This will ensure high availability as well as the disaster-recovery scenario. This scenario has been recommended because if one availability domain goes down, the other availability domain will ensure that the systems are available and the data is secure. The elite high performing network arrangement between Oracle Cloud Infrastructure availability domains empowers this deployment.

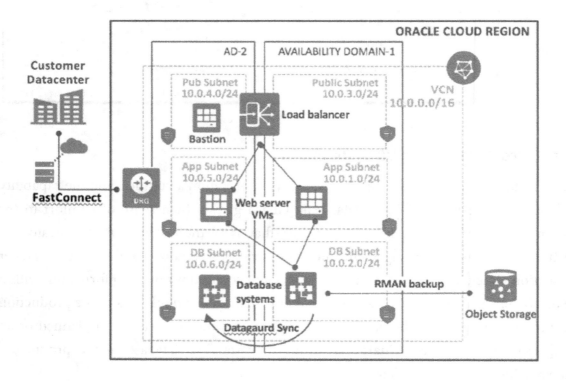

Oracle Data Guard keeps up the standby database by the transmission and the application of redo logs on to the standby from the primary database.

On the off chance that the primary database ends up inaccessible, Database Administrator will perform the role change of changing standby database to the primary database.

The following possibilities exist with Data Guard setup to help high accessibility:

- **Switchover:** It does the reversing of the primary and standby database roles. In this scenario, both the production and the standby database play their role in the Data Guard setup and interchange themselves. A switchover guarantees no loss of information. A switchover plays very handily when there is planned downtime for production maintenance activity.

- **Failover:** It transitions the Data Guard standby database into the primary database after the current production database crashes or becomes inaccessible. A failover may bring about certain data loss if the Data Guard has been setup for Maximum Performance protection mode.

- **Reinstate:** Reinstates a primary production database into standby database in a Data Guard setup. The reinstate command can be helpful in bringing back the failed database into the primary role after the issue with the database has been fixed.

FASTCONNECT IN OCI

Oracle Cloud Infrastructure FastConnect gives a simple method to make a dedicated, private connection between Oracle Cloud Infrastructure and the customer's datacentre. FastConnect gives higher-transfer speed choices, and an increasingly dependable and predictable network connectivity experience contrasted with the normal internet-based connectivity.

FastConnect Can Be Used For

With FastConnect, you can utilise private peering, public peering, or both.

Private peering: To broaden the current infrastructure into a virtual cloud network (VCN) in Oracle Cloud Infrastructure (for instance, to perform a lift and shift of the databases or application, to setup a hybrid cloud such as production on-premise and

Disaster recovery on the cloud). The communication that is established utilises IPv4 private addresses (the regularly used RFC 1918).

Public peering: This is to access the Oracle Cloud Infrastructure without utilizing the web. For instance, Object Storage, the Oracle Cloud Infrastructure Console and APIs, or public load balancers in the VCN. IPv4 public IP addresses are used to establish communication in the connectivity. The best part is that With FastConnect, that traffic goes over your private physical connectivity and if the FastConnect is not used the traffic bound for public IP would be directed over the web.

There are three connectivity models using which the **physical connectivity** can be established.

Utilizing an Oracle Network Provider or Exchange Partner

You can build up a FastConnect connection from the customers' on-premises datacentre or even a remote datacentre into the datacentre where the Oracle Cloud resources are provisioned by taking the services from any of Oracle's FastConnect partner channels. Oracle has integrated the FastConnect service with a geographically assorted arrangement of IP VPN and Ethernet Network suppliers and Cloud Exchanges to make it simple so that connection can be established with Oracle FastConnect partners.

This availability model is reasonable in the event that you intend to utilise, or are as of now utilizing network connectivity services from any Oracle FastConnect accomplice. It is also recommended that redundant cloud connectivity be established by requesting the same from the Oracle FastConnect partner, because it will assist in case if there is a failure in the primary connection.

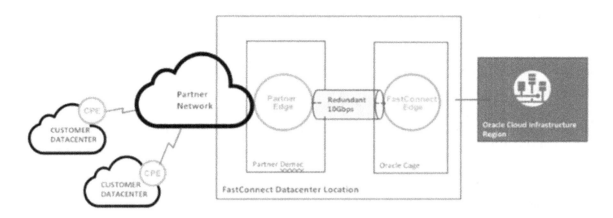

Direct to Oracle Datacentre Colocation

In the event that you have bought colocation space from a datacentre supplier, you can utilise Oracle FastConnect to build up connectivity from the network equipment in the colocation facility to the Oracle Cloud services that are present in the specified location. Oracle will give you a letter of approval (LOA) that the datacentre provider will require to set up a direct cross-connect into Oracle's FastConnect edge devices.

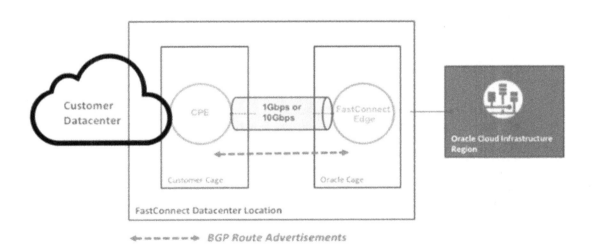

This availability model is appropriate in the event that you as of now have a presence at an Oracle FastConnect location or are hoping to set up a colocation presence there. Two such connections can be arranged into a datacentre in the event that the redundancy is required.

Direct connectivity with Oracle: Assistance from a third-party network carrier to establish dedicated circuits

A FastConnect connection can be established from your remote datacentre into Oracle's datacentre where your Cloud resources are provisioned, by requesting a Private or dedicated Circuit from a third-party Network carries that is not an Oracle FastConnect Partner. This provider, who is an MPLS VPN provider, will be in charge of the whole physical connection between your on-premises network and Oracle's FastConnect edge devices including the final connectivity inside Oracle's datacentre. Oracle will give you an LOA that should be given to the third-party Network provider who will assist in the whole arrangement for establishing the network. You can arrange two such circuits from your Network provider into the Oracle datacentre in the event that you need redundancy.

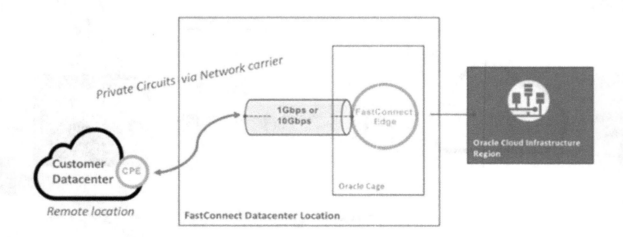

BEST PRACTICES FOR DISASTER RECOVERY ON OCI

Disaster recovery (DR) is the way toward shielding your applications from a catastrophe. A disaster can be whatever puts your applications in danger, from network outages to hardware failures to catastrophic events. At the point when an unanticipated disaster occurs, a well-architected DR plan plays a key role in the applications to recover as fast as could reasonably be expected and to keep on giving services to the customers. Oracle Cloud Infrastructure has the capability of providing the infrastructure that is highly available and scalable and gives the enabling power for disaster-recovery setup for the applications to be dependable, secure, and quick.

We shall discuss the best practices for the design and implementation for securing the applications for disaster on Oracle Cloud Infrastructure.

The concept of DR has two important concepts linked with it—Recovery Time Objective (RTO) and Recovery Point Objective (RPO).

The **RTO** is the objective time that is required for the restoration of the application functionality after a debacle occurs. The objective is to quantify how rapidly the application can be recouped from a debacle. Typically, if the criticality of the applications is more, RTO is lower.

The **RPO** is the acceptable time limit of lost data that the applications can endure. RPO is about how much information the applications in the enterprise can afford to lose in a disaster situation.

To setup a DR plan that ensures the endurance of the applications after a disaster scenario and is additionally financially effective as well, RTO and RPO should also be considered. The best disaster-recovery plan should ensure that RTO and RPO objectives could be accomplished to recover the applications adequately from a disaster situation.

Key concepts to be understood

An Oracle Cloud Infrastructure region is a localised area within a specific geography, which have many availability domains, which in turn have fault domains within them.

Regions are free of other regions and can be isolated by tremendous distances over nations or even continents. Applications can be deployed in different regions to alleviate the danger of region wide unforeseen circumstances, for example, huge climatic changes or seismic tremors.

An **availability domain** is one or more datacentres that are situated within a specific region. Availability domains are separated from one another, fault tolerant, and far-fetched to flop at the same time. Because availability domains do not share physical hardware, for example, power or cooling, or the internal availability domain network, a failure that effects one availability domain is probably not going to affect others. Availability domains in a region are associated with one another by a low-latency and high bandwidth networks.

Hardware and infrastructure grouped within an availability domain is called **fault domain**. Every availability domain contains three fault domains. Fault domains give the capability of distributing the instances so they are not on the same physical infrastructure inside the same availability domain. Therefore, equipment failures or any maintenance activity that happens in a particular fault domain does not affect the instances in another fault domain.

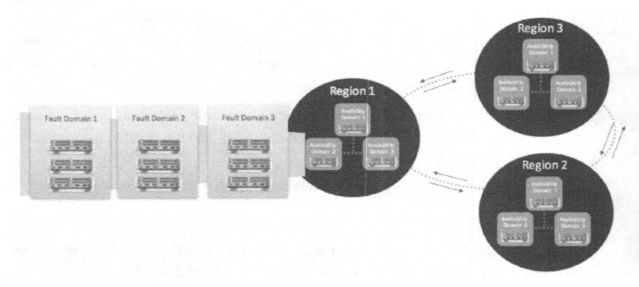

Recommended Strategies

To shield the applications from potential disasters, it is critical to setup the application deployment methodology based on the RTO and RPO information.

Single Region with One Availability Domain

Applications can be setup over multiple fault domains in the case of regions that have a single availability domain so that it would be helpful in shielding the applications from unforeseen hardware failures or outages for the maintenance activity. On the off chance that the whole availability domain encounters a disaster, this kind of setup does not help in giving the protection. It is recommended to have replication to a remote region for DR in the case of such scenarios where the region has only one availability domain within it.

For instance, you may back up block volumes to the remote regions that are kept far off from the primary region. If a disaster affects the primary region, databases and the applications can be built in the remote regions if the block volume-backups are replicated to another region at regular intervals. The volumes that were backed in the remote region can assist in re-establishing the applications without significant data loss.

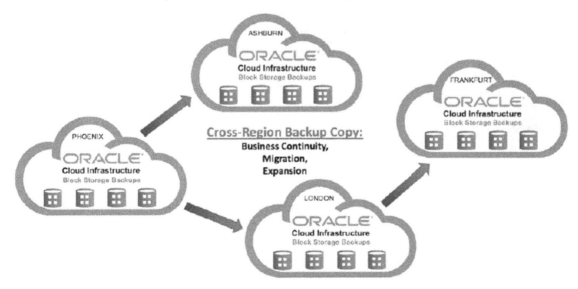

Single Region with Multiple Availability Domains

Based upon the criticality of the applications, the applications can be deployed in a single region. Because each region has multiple availability domains, the applications can be deployed over multiple availability domains, so that the application will not be impacted even if there is a disaster or a planned downtime in a particular availability domain. It is suggested for utilizing the Oracle Cloud Infrastructure Load Balancer services in the DR configuration to limit the downtime to the applications. In the event that the application stack contains a database, it is recommended that a standby database be setup in a different availability domain from the primary database and a Data Guard can also be established between them for further protection. In addition, the database can also be backed up to Oracle Cloud Infrastructure Object Storage for further protection of customer data.

The picture below illustrates a deployment where there are multiple availability domains within a single region.

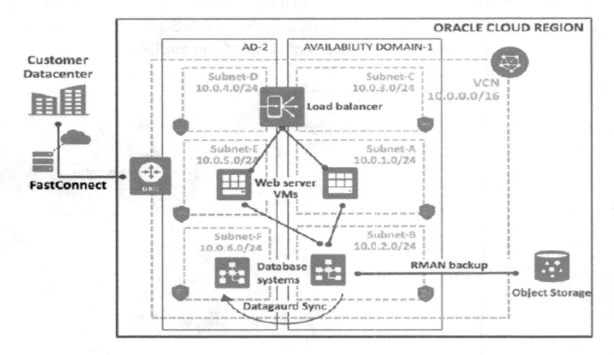

Cross-Region

A cross-region setup has to be considered as a disaster-recovery solution for the deployment of mission critical applications. Oracle Cloud Infrastructure gives low-latency and high performing bandwidths between Oracle Cloud Infrastructure regions. VCN peering can be utilised to set up secure and reliable connectivity between various VCNs among regions.

"rsync" can be used to asynchronously copy the file system or snapshot data to another region and this will help in achieving cross-regional data protection.

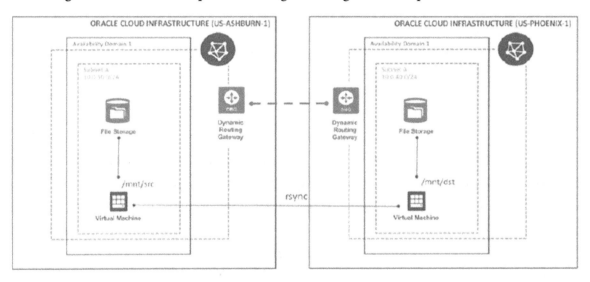

As shown in the picture below, the out-of-the-box capabilities can be achieved from the Oracle Database on Oracle Cloud Infrastructure.

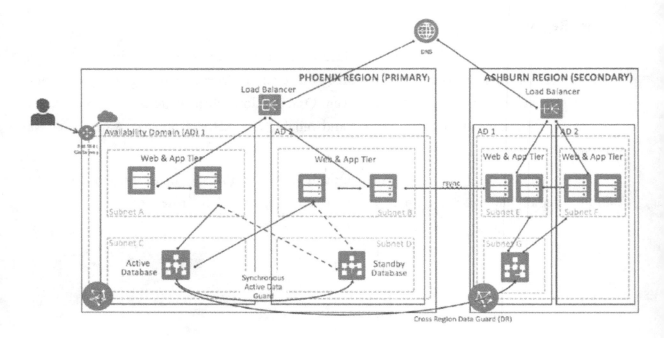

Each of the application tier nodes and the web tier nodes speaks with one of the database tier nodes. Oracle Cloud Infrastructure supports RAC and Exadata, so high accessibility can be achieved within a single availability domain. In the event that failure happens in the database, Active Data Guard is utilised to synchronise to an identical database in the other availability domain, which resides within the same region or across regions.

Recommended Practice for OCI in Data Guard Configuration

The below picture shows the recommended configuration for Oracle Data Guard on Oracle Cloud Infrastructure:

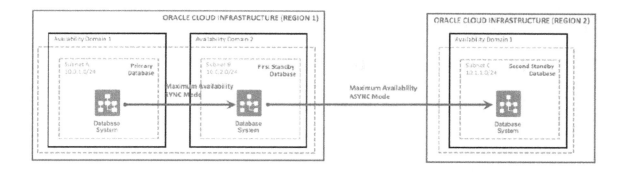

The above shown setup offers the below advantages:

- No loss of data inside a region.
- No overhead on the production database for the maintenance of standbys in another region.
- Option for the configuration of lagging on the DR site if necessary for business reasons.
- Option to design numerous standbys in various regions with no extra overhead on the production database.

In conclusion, all three Data Guard setups - Maximum Protection, Maximum Availability & Maximum Performance are completely supported by Oracle Cloud Infrastructure. Furthermore, because of a risk factor for production outage, Oracle does not recommend utilizing the Maximum Protection mode for the Data Guard setup. Oracle Cloud Infrastructure suggests utilizing the Maximum Availability mode in SYNC mode between two availability domains within the same region and utilizing the Maximum Availability mode in ASYNC mode between two different regions. This configuration will provide you with the best RTO and RPO without any loss of data. Oracle Cloud Infrastructure recommends the setup of this design in daisy-chain mode, in which the primary database ships redo logs to the first standby database in another availability domain in SYNC mode and after that, the first standby database transports the redo logs to another region in ASYNC mode. This strategy guarantees that the production database is not doing the twofold work of shipping redo logs, which can lead to a compromise with the performance in the production environment.

THREAT TO APPLICATIONS ON THE CLOUD

Oracle and KPMG have done a study and come up with a Cloud Threat Report 2019 that looks at developing cybersecurity challenges and dangers that organizations are looking as they embrace cloud services at a quickening pace. The report gives pioneers the world over and across the industries with significant bits of knowledge and proposals for how they can guarantee that cybersecurity is a basic business-empowering influence.

With cloud benefits now important to all areas of business activities, the interest for speed and dexterity is combined with the desire for more prominent security. Truth be told, 73% of study respondents demonstrate the cloud offers a more secure environment than they can give on-premises. This observation has brought about proceeded and developing cloud reception: a very clear number of businesses have expanded the measure of business-critical data they host in the cloud.

For every one of the worries about the quickening pace of progress, rising innovation improvements keep on fortifying cybersecurity teams' capacity to help the business. The capacity to help address vulnerabilities consequently is energising.

Machine Learning, AI the speed at which we can execute security processes– it's everything bringing about less downtime for certain clients what's more, the upgraded capacity for all to utilise cybersecurity as a business-empowering agent. These services and advancements are developing to the point that we can truly begin to make progress, mitigating points of exposure, with regards to business strategy.

Cloud Services Have Become More dependent and business-critical:

Enterprises are progressively depending upon cloud services for business activities and trust them to store sensitive information.

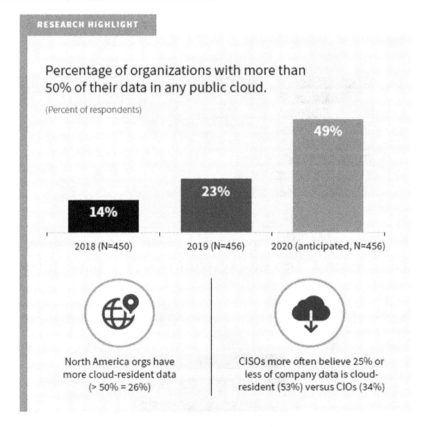

The continuous expansion in the cloud area is that cloud services are turning into the primary information store for many enterprises. Indeed, over half North American organizations that took part in the survey done by Oracle & KPMG have 26% or a greater amount of their information in the cloud, and almost half (49%) of all respondents hope to store most of their data in a public cloud by 2020 .

The Dependency on Cloud Services Is increasing Cybersecurity Challenges.

An extended assault surface adds to alert storms and the skills shortage, yet focus and financing have improved.

Of the considerable number of difficulties related to securing cloud services, maybe the most critical is the degree of confusion around the shared responsibility security model.

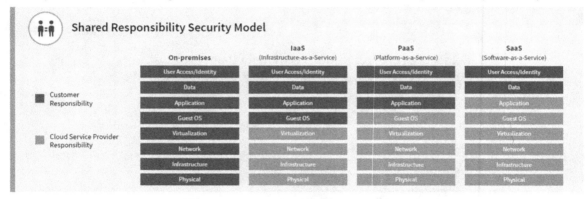

As per the survey done, the respondents had different opinions for different cloud offerings, regarding the shared responsibility security model as shown below:

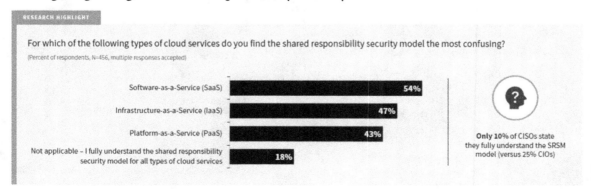

CISOs are especially mindful of the cloud security visibility gap, with 38% referring to the failure of system security controls to give visibility into public cloud workloads as their top cloud security challenge. The other challenges faced by respondents have been highlighted below:

RESEARCH HIGHLIGHT

What are the biggest cybersecurity challenges currently experienced by your organization today?

(Percent of respondents, N=456, three responses accepted, five most frequently reported challenges shown)

Challenge	Percent
Detecting and reacting to security incidents in the cloud	33%
Lack of skills and qualified staff	29%
Lack of alignment between security operations and IT operations teams	27%
The unauthorized use of cloud services	26%
Lack of visibility across our data center and endpoint attack surface	24%

The respondents in the survey have highlighted that the shortage of talent is in the area of cybersecurity as shown below:

Of the respondents to the Oracle/KPMG research review, 30% referred to the failure of their network security controls to give visibility into cloud-occupant server workloads a top cloud security concern.

The most commonly mentioned cloud security challenge was the configuration management, particularly when considering the immutable nature of production cloud resident server workloads, which are normally not patches or modified. It is in this setting the highest level of research respondents referred to keeping up secure setups for server workloads as one of their top cloud security issues (39%).

IS YOUR DATA SECURE?

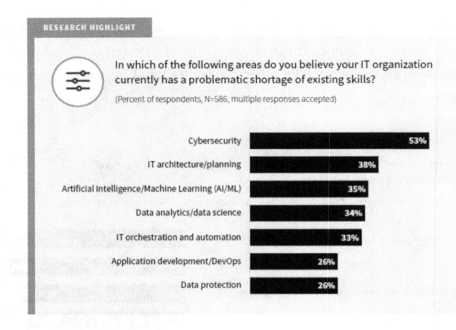

RESEARCH HIGHLIGHT

In which of the following areas do you believe your IT organization currently has a problematic shortage of existing skills?

(Percent of respondents, N=586, multiple responses accepted)

Cybersecurity	53%
IT architecture/planning	38%
Artificial Intelligence/Machine Learning (AI/ML)	35%
Data analytics/data science	34%
IT orchestration and automation	33%
Application development/DevOps	26%
Data protection	26%

RESEARCH HIGHLIGHT

Which of the following represents the biggest cloud security challenges for your organization?

(Percent of respondents, N=456, five responses accepted, seven most frequently reported challenges shown)

Maintaining secure configurations for our cloud-resident workloads	39%
Satisfying our security team that our public cloud infrastructure is secure	38%
Maintaining strong and consistent security across our own data center and public cloud environments in use	38%
Cloud-related security event management challenges	37%
Aligning regulatory compliance requirements with my organization's cloud strategy	30%
Inability for existing network-security controls to provide visibility into public cloud-resident workloads	30%
Inability to automate the application of security controls due to the lack of integration with DevOps tools	30%

132

While the organizations in the survey reported encountering a wide scope of cyber-attacks in the course of the most recent two years, email phishing was the top spot as the assault vector that was experienced regularly during that period, a questionable qualification certainly. The continuous high episode pace of email phishing is an update that digital enemies will default to those techniques that have demonstrated powerful and influence them in new manners.

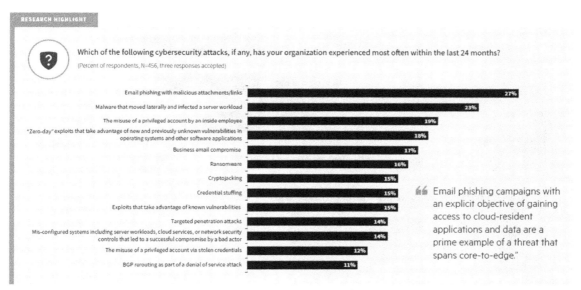

Almost half (49%) of the businesses in the current year's investigation report a traded off the third-party was the reason for presenting malware, with another 46% detailing that an outsider was the reason for unapproved access to information and 39% sharing that they lost information as a consequence of an outsider. The loss of information because of third-party access is progressively intense for small and medium organizations, with 44% of those businesses announcing this result, characteristic of the less procedures and controls employed by smaller organizations. These look into discoveries feature that more thoughtfulness regarding third-party risk management is required.

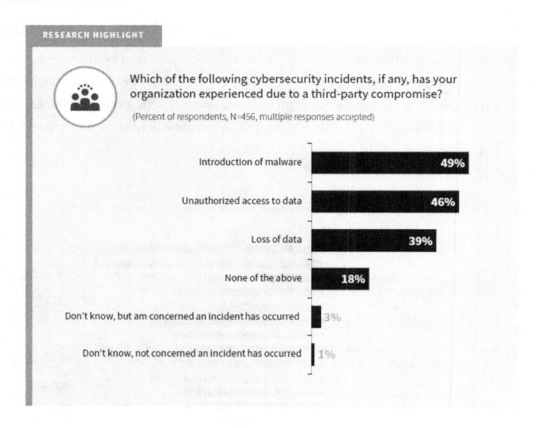

RESEARCH HIGHLIGHT

Which of the following cybersecurity incidents, if any, has your organization experienced due to a third-party compromise?

(Percent of respondents, N=456, multiple responses accepted)

Introduction of malware	49%
Unauthorized access to data	46%
Loss of data	39%
None of the above	18%
Don't know, but am concerned an incident has occurred	3%
Don't know, not concerned an incident has occurred	1%

A few patches require a reboot, which would affect accessibility furthermore, the settled upon service level agreement (SLA) IT has with the business for specific applications, the most referred-to purpose behind deferring patching, as referred to by 46% of the participating organizations. As a result, some unmistakably conflate the operational significance of very critical applications with the need to secure those systems from the trade-off through increasingly proactive patching, particularly when various patches are in the line. Software compatibility was about as normal an explanation to postpone patching, a bi-directional impediment when the current version of a software package does not yet support the version of the operating system to be patched or the other way around. There are additionally process deterrents as for approval cycles for change control and the actuality that the risk associated with certain vulnerabilities is to such an extent that IT does not see the patching as warranted.

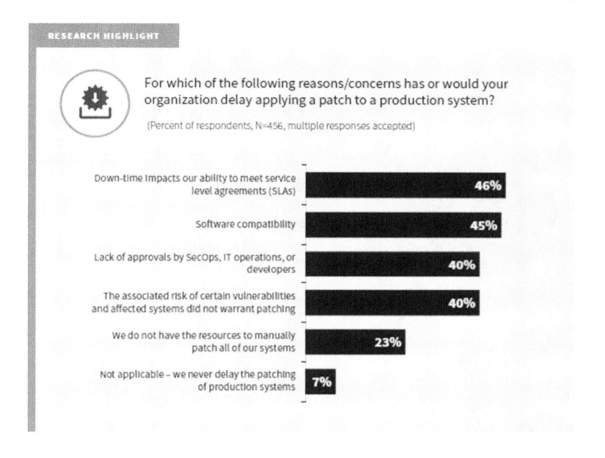

Businesses have a strong interest in Automated Patching to Eliminate Operational Obstacle. The following most significant cybersecurity improvement step, after penetration testing and progressively continuous patching, is automated patching. The utilization of automated patching is now in play for 43% of the inquired about organizations, with half of bigger organizations previously doing as such. In addition, a striking 46% more intend to actualise automated patching throughout the next two years or so. IT and security groups are obviously utilizing automation both to address interminable operational issues what's more, to improve their organization's cybersecurity position.

IS YOUR DATA SECURE?

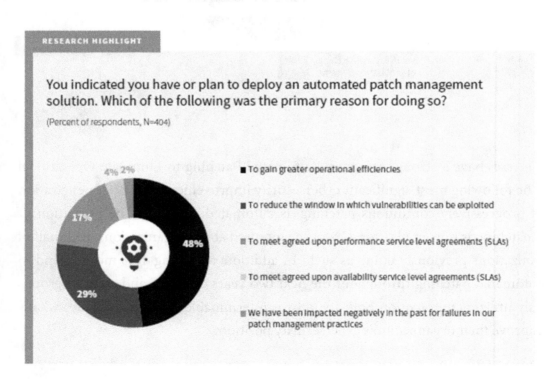

RESEARCH HIGHLIGHT

Have or does your organization plan to deploy a solution that automates patch management for production environments?

(Percent of respondents, N=456)

- 43% Yes, we have implemented automated patch management
- 46% Yes, we plan to implement automated patch management in the next 12-24 months
- 8% No, but we are interested in automated patch management
- 3% No plans or interest

RESEARCH HIGHLIGHT

You indicated you have or plan to deploy an automated patch management solution. Which of the following was the primary reason for doing so?

(Percent of respondents, N=404)

- 48% To gain greater operational efficiencies
- 29% To reduce the window in which vulnerabilities can be exploited
- 17% To meet agreed upon performance service level agreements (SLAs)
- 4% To meet agreed upon availability service level agreements (SLAs)
- 2% We have been impacted negatively in the past for failures in our patch management practices

136

IT is seeking other options to passwords. Cloud and Mobility Are Complicating IAM methodologies. Management of passwords is another long-standing issue that affects not just IT teams with steady demands to reset forgotten passwords, yet in addition end-users as well. Past such bothers, awful hackers have turned out to be skilled at taking credentials through an assortment of strategies and techniques. Shown below is the feedback from the respondents on the concept of password and its replacement with another form of authentication.

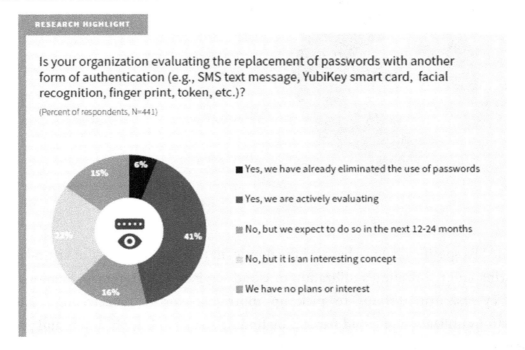

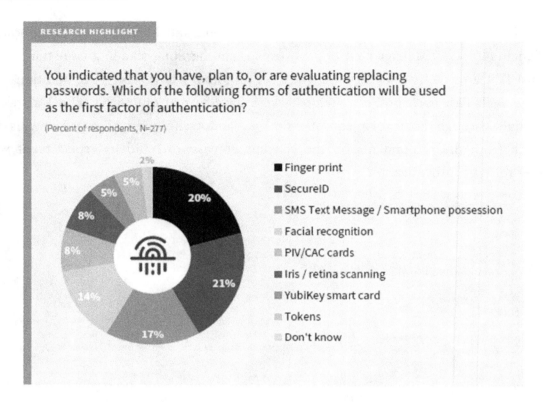

You indicated that you have, plan to, or are evaluating replacing passwords. Which of the following forms of authentication will be used as the first factor of authentication?

(Percent of respondents, N=277)

- Finger print — 20%
- SecureID — 21%
- SMS Text Message / Smartphone possession — 17%
- Facial recognition — 14%
- PIV/CAC cards — 8%
- Iris / retina scanning — 8%
- YubiKey smart card — 5%
- Tokens — 5%
- Don't know — 2%

CASBs specifically have become the dominant focal point as a lot of critical controls for securing an organization's utilization of cloud services. CASB implementations permit IT and cybersecurity groups to pick up more noteworthy perceivability into their organizations utilization of cloud services by finding shadow IT applications and providing details regarding their related hazard, classifying sensitive information as the reason for applying data loss prevention (DLP) policies, and recognising both in-flight dangers and malware put stored with cloud services.

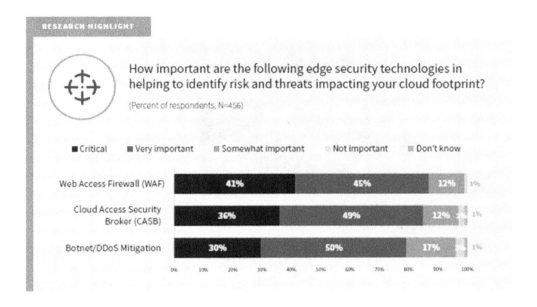

SQL INJECTION

SQL Injection (SQLi) is a sort of an infusion assault that makes it probable to execute malicious SQL queries. These queries control a database server behind a web application. Assailants can utilize SQL Injection vulnerabilities to sidestep application security protocols. They can circumvent authentication and authorization of a website page or web application and try to get the data from the database. They can likewise utilise SQL Injection to insert, change, and erase data in the database.

An SQL Injection vulnerability may influence any website or web application that uses any database, for example, MySQL, Postgres, MongoDB, Oracle, SQL Server, or others. Hackers may utilise it to increase unapproved access to sensitive information such as client data, individual information, trade secrets, intellectual property and the sky is the limit from there. SQL Injection assaults are one of the most seasoned, most pervasive, and most hazardous web application vulnerabilities. The OWASP association (Open Web Application Security Project) records infusions in their OWASP Top 10 2017 report as one of the main dangers to web application security.

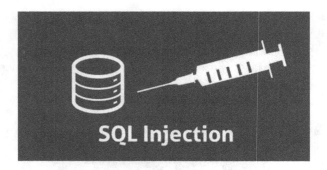

Purpose of SQL Injection attack

To make an attack using SQL Injection, an aggressor should initially discover vulnerable user inputs inside the website page or web application. A page or web application that has an SQL Injection vulnerability uses such user input straightforwardly in an SQL inquiry. The aggressor can make input content. Such content is regularly called a malicious payload and is the key piece of the assault. After the hacker sends this bad content, noxious SQL commands are executed in the database.

As we all know, SQL structured query language that was intended to manage information kept in relational databases. SQL can be utilised to perform DML operations such as insert, update and delete information. Many web applications and sites store every one of the information in SQL databases. At times, you can likewise utilise SQL commands to run operating system commands as well. Along these lines, an effective SQL Injection assault can have intense outcomes.

- ☐ Attackers can utilise SQL Injections to discover the credentials of different users in the database. They would then be able to mimic these user IDs. The imitated clients might be a database administrator with all the required database privileges that has complete access to the database including starting and stopping the database.
- ☐ SQL allows you to choose and yield information from the database. An SQL Injection defenselessness could enable the hacker to increase total access to all information in a database server.

- ☐ SQL, likewise, gives you the platform to alert information in a database and include new information. For instance, in a monetary application, an aggressor could utilise SQL Injection to adjust balances, void transactions, or move cash to their own accounts.

- ☐ You can utilize SQL to erase records from a database, even drop tables. Regardless of whether the database administrator has taken the backup of the database or not, erasure of information could influence application accessibility until the database is restored. Additionally, backups may not cover the latest information.

- ☐ In some database servers, you can get to the working Operating System that is behind the database utilizing the database server. This might be purposeful or inadvertent. In such a case, a hacker could utilise an SQL Injection as the underlying vector and afterwards assault the internal network of the organization behind a firewall.

In conclusion, we can understand the hazardous effects of SQL Injection and the harm it can cause to the databases and in turn to the enterprise at large. Security Managers are very keen to keep SQL Injections away from the systems and they try everything possible to achieve it from the security angle.

One of the key methods to avert SQL Injection assaults is input validation and parametrised queries including already prepared statements. The application code ought to never utilise the input directly. The technical developer must purify all information, not just web structure sources of information, for example, login forms. They should evacuate potential malicious code components, for example, single quotes. It is additionally a smart thought to switch off the visibility of database errors on the production databases. Database errors can be utilised with SQL Injection to pick up data about the database.

Reference:

https://www.ycdsb.ca/sps/2016/09/04/highlights-of-key-policy-procedures/

MacAfee Blog

https://cloud.oracle.com/opc/paas/datasheets/Cloud-Security-Essentials-CASB-Requirements_take2_Jan+2019.pdf

https://www.cloudcodes.com/blog/cloud-access-security-brokers-solutions.html

https://blogs.oracle.com/cloudsecurity/oracle-data-safe-five-ways-to-help-protect-your-digital-assets

https://medium.com/@isuruj/introduction-to-encryption-4b810996a871

Best Practices for Deploying High Availability Architecture on Oracle Cloud Infrastructure

ORACLE AND KPMG CLOUD THREAT REPORT 2019

https://medium.com/@charithra/introduction-to-sql-injections-8c806537cf5d

3

BUSTED MYTHS AROUND SECURITY ON THE CLOUD

IT IS TIME TO UNDERSTAND THE GROUND REALITY & GET OVER THE MYTHS ABOUT CLOUD SECURITY

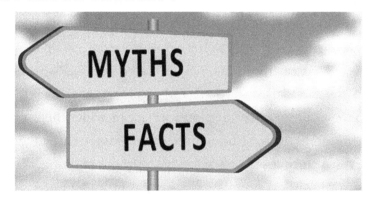

Cloud is a buzzword in the Information Technology industry these days and many businesses are heading to the cloud. It is just not about the migration of the database and the application to the cloud, but it is also about maintaining the security of the customers' data. The cloud concept has seen an enormous growth in the last few years, which in turn has made the key decision-makers in both the public and private sector take a decision to adopt the cloud technology. Having said the above statement, still all is not well with the decision-making as there is still a lot of hesitancy in the Information Technology world as they have a lot of myths lingering around in their minds with regards to a key factor such as "Security". These myths, so-called misconceptions that are present in the minds are a hindrance and one of the main reasons if any business has not moved to the cloud yet. The cloud Service providers are also doing their bit in clearing the doubts related to security. Every cloud provider is trying to enhance its security levels on the cloud, as they feel that better security can be a good marketing factor for them to attract businesses to their cloud. A lot of myths have already been debunked, but still a few remain and these have been discussed in this blog.

Myth 1: The cloud is not secure as my on-premise

Reality: The security on the cloud is one of the biggest challenges for any cloud service provider. This challenge pushes every cloud service provider to enhance the security with stringent policies coupled with the latest technology in the security space. The better security the cloud service provider gives to the customer for its data, the chances are better for the cloud service provider to attract the customer to its cloud. Therefore, they have been investing billions of dollars in securing the infrastructure in their datacentres that host the cloud servers and they attract the best talents who have expertise in cloud security and are certified in security-related certifications, which are recognised worldwide. Furthermore, the data that is on the cloud is encrypted and also few cloud service providers sign a memorandum with the customer that the cloud service provider themselves will not be able to access the data. In comparison, although security measures are taken by Infrastructure managers to secure the on-premises datacentre with proper auditing, the quality of security on the cloud is superior to the on-premises for the reasons mentioned above.

Myth 2: Cloud is a synonym for virtualization

Reality: No doubt, the concept of virtualization is used in clouds, but that does not mean the virtualization is the same as the cloud. Cloud is a step ahead of virtualization. A huge range of service-based functionalities and computing capabilities form the cloud. Clouds give the additional benefits of self-service access, scale-up of hardware based on the need, and allocation of resources dynamically which makes it stand out from the normal and the traditional concept of virtualization.

Myth 3: Cloud is made up of one single size and it fits all

Reality: Cloud is a bigger concept and different customers choose differently among the available options on the cloud. Cloud has three models available such as Software as a Service (SaaS), Platform as a Service (PaaS), and IaaS. Each of these has its own pros and cons and the right decision has to be made before migrating to the Cloud. Cloud gives you the benefit of choosing the memory, storage and the CPUs based on your requirement. Therefore, its different size for different customers based on the need.

Myth 4: When you move to the cloud, you should be locked only with a single CSP

Reality: Cloud is also a very competitive market and the cloud service providers (CSP) ensure to attract the customers to their cloud by giving different cloud offerings at better quality, security and reasonable rates. The best and the most prominent cloud providers give the option of public, private and hybrid cloud to their customers. There is also a possibility that the customer can decide which application should be migrated to Oracle Cloud and which one to AWS or Microsoft Azure. This myth is debunked with a practical example with an ERP software such as Oracle E-Business Suite. The application in Oracle ERP can be deployed in Microsoft Azure and the database in Oracle Cloud Infrastructure on the Oracle Cloud. With the help of this cross-cloud connectivity, customers benefit low-latency, high throughput connectivity and enjoy the best of both the clouds.

Myth 5: You have to move in entirety to the cloud

Reality: Hybrid cloud is a very important concept in the cloud world. The Information technology manager can have the challenge of moving all applications to the cloud-based on factors such as costs, security and compliance issues, legacy applications etc. Hybrid cloud answers these issues, as there is an option of having some applications on-premise and moving a few to the public cloud. Based on the data and compliance issues in the financial sector, IT managers in the banking domain prefer to have some applications on-premise or within the cloud at their own datacentre. There is also a possibility of having the cloud at the customer's datacentre as well and Oracle Cloud gives the facility, which is known as Cloud at the customer by delivering the cloud to the customer's datacentre.

SECURITY RELATED TO THE ORACLE DATABASE

INTRODUCTION TO ORACLE DATABASE SECURITY

Oracle Database provides a rich set of default security features to manage user accounts, authentication, privileges, application security, encryption, network traffic, and auditing.

Oracle Database Security

Oracle Database Security

You can use Oracle Database features to configure security in several areas for your Oracle Database installation.

The areas in which you can configure security are as follows:

Secure Parameter

Security Parameter checklist provides guidance on configuring parameters in a secure manner by adhering to and recommending industry-standard and advisable "security practices" for operational database deployments. Secure Parameter list provides detailed information

Network Data Encryption

You can configure native Oracle Net Services data encryption and integrity for both servers and clients, which are described in Configuring Oracle Database Native Network Encryption and Data Integrity.

Virtual Private Database

A Virtual Private Database policy dynamically embeds a WHERE predicate into SQL statements the user issues. Using Oracle Virtual Private Database to Control Data Access, describes how to create and manage Virtual Private Database policies. The chapter VPD provides detailed information.

Thin JDBC Client Network Configuration

You can configure thin JDBC clients to securely connect to Oracle databases. Configuring the Thin JDBC Client Network, provides detailed information.

Strong Authentication

You can configure your databases to use strong authentication with Oracle authentication adapters that support various third-party authentication services, including SSL with digital certificates.

Oracle Database provides the following strong authentication support:

- Centralised authentication and single sign-on
- Kerberos – Remote Authentication Dial-in User Service (RADIUS)
- SSL
- The following chapters cover strong authentication:
- Configuration and Administration Tools Overview
- Strong Authentication Administration Tools
- Integrating Authentication Devices Using RADIUS
- Configuring Kerberos Authentication
- Configuring SSL Authentication
- Configuring RADIUS Authentication
- Customizing the Use of Strong Authentication
- Oracle Database FIPS 140
- Configuring Multiple Authentication Methods and Disabling Oracle Strong Authentication

Oracle Utility to Manage Wallet

The security provided by public key infrastructure (PKI) depends on how effectively you store, manage, and validate your PKI credentials. Wallet owners and security administrators use Oracle Wallet Manager to manage and edit the security credentials in their Oracle wallets. The orapki utility manages certificate revocation lists (CRLs), creates and manages Oracle wallets, and creates signed certificates. More detail provided on this in the following chapter.

- ☐ Using Oracle Wallet Manager
- ☐ Orapki utility

CONFIGURATION AND ADMINISTRATION TOOLS OVERVIEW

You can use a set of strong authentication administration tools for native network encryption and PKI credentials.

- ☐ Introduction
- ☐ Strong Authentication Configuration Tools
- ☐ PKI Credentials Management Tools
- ☐ Conclusion

Introduction

The configuration and administration tools manage the encryption, integrity (checksumming), and strong authentication methods for Oracle Net Services. Strong authentication method configuration can include third-party software, as is the case for Kerberos or RADIUS, or it may entail configuring and managing a PKI for using digital certificates with SSL.

Strong Authentication Configuration Tools

Oracle Net Services can encrypt data using standard encryption algorithms, and for strong authentication methods, such as Kerberos, RADIUS, and SSL.

- ☐ About Oracle Net Manager
- ☐ Kerberos Adapter Command-Line Utilities

About Oracle Net Manager

Oracle Net Manager configures Oracle Net Services for an Oracle home on a local client or server host.

Although you can use Oracle Net Manager, a graphical user interface tool, to configure Oracle Net Services, such as naming, listeners, and general network settings, it also enables you to configure the following features, which use the Oracle Net protocol:

- ☐ Strong authentication (Kerberos, RADIUS, and SSL)
- ☐ Native network encryption (RC4, DES, Triple-DES, and AES)
- ☐ Checksumming for data integrity (MD5, SHA-1, SHA-2)

Kerberos Adapter Command-Line Utilities

The Kerberos adapter provides command-line utilities that obtain, cache, display, and remove Kerberos credentials.

Okinit - Obtains Kerberos tickets from the Key Distribution Centre (KDC) and caches them in the user's credential cache

Oklist - Displays a list of Kerberos tickets in the specified credential cache

Okdstry - Removes Kerberos credentials from the specified credential cache

Okcreate - Automates the creation of keytabs from either the KDC or a service endpoint

Note:

The Cybersafe adapter is not supported beginning with this release. You should use Oracle's Kerberos adapter in its place. Kerberos authentication with the Cybersafe KDC (Trust Broker) continues to be supported when using the Kerberos adapter.

PKI Credentials Management Tools

The security provided by PKI depends on how effectively you store, manage, and validate your PKI credentials.

- ☐ About Oracle Wallet Manager
- ☐ About the orapki Utility

About Oracle Wallet Manager

Wallet owners and security administrators use Oracle Wallet Manager to manage and edit the security credentials in their Oracle wallets.

A wallet is a password-protected container that is used to store authentication and signing credentials, including private keys, certificates, and trusted certificates needed by SSL. You can use Oracle Wallet Manager to perform the following tasks:

- ☐ Create public and private key pairs
- ☐ Store and manage user credentials
- ☐ Generate certificate requests
- ☐ Store and manage certificate authority certificates (root key certificate and certificate chain)
- ☐ Upload and download wallets to and from an LDAP directory
- ☐ Create wallets to store hardware security module credentials

About the Orapki Utility

The orapki utility manages CRLs, creates and manages Oracle wallets, and creates signed certificates.

The basic syntax for this command-line utility is as follows:

orapki *module command -option_1 argument … -option_n argument*

For example, the following command lists all CRLs in the CRL subtree in an instance of Oracle Internet Directory that is installed on machine1.us.example.com and that uses port 389:

orapki crl list -ldap machine1.us.example.com:389

Conclusion

In this chapter, we have discussed multiple tools like Oracle net manager and Oracle wallet manager and third-party authentication method like Kerberos. In the latter chapter, we will discuss more details regarding the configuration and administration of these tools.

SECURITY PARAMETER CHECKLIST

Introduction

Security Parameter checklist provides guidance on configuring parameters in a secure manner by adhering to and recommending industry-standard and advisable "security practices" for operational database deployments.

Before looking at the more detailed checklist: consider all paths the data travels and assess the threats that impact on each path and node. Then, take steps to lessen or eliminate both the threats and the consequences of a successful breach of security. Monitoring and auditing to detect either increased threat levels or successful penetration increases the likelihood of preventing and minimising security losses. Here you are going to see the details on parameters which are used in the secure environment and it is a good practice to enable security parameter to get better security. In the following topic, we will understand what parameter is used to prevent action from privileged user, non-privileged user, network problems and audit queries.

- ☐ Initialization Parameters Used for Privilege Security
- ☐ Initialization Parameters Used for Installation and Configuration Security
- ☐ Parameters Used to Secure User Accounts
- ☐ Initialization Parameters Used for Network Security
- ☐ Initialization Parameters Used for Auditing

We are going to see one by one of these checklists.

Initialization Parameters Used for Privilege Security

Initialization Parameter	Default Setting
OS_ROLES	FALSE
MAX_ENABLED_ROLES	30
REMOTE_OS_ROLES	FALSE
SQL92_SECURITY	FALSE

OS_ROLES

Determines whether the operating system identifies and manages the roles of each user.

REMOTE_OS_ROLES

Specifies whether operating system roles are allowed for remote clients. The default value, FALSE, causes Oracle to identify and manage roles for remote clients.

MAX_ENABLED_ROLES

Specifies the maximum number of database roles that users can enable, including roles contained within other roles.

SQL92_SECURITY

Specifies whether users must be granted the SELECT object privilege to execute UPDATE or DELETE statements.

Initialization Parameters Used for Installation and Configuration Security

Initialization Parameter	Default Setting
SEC_RETURN_SERVER_RELEASE_BANNER	FALSE
O7_DICTIONARY_ACCESSIBILITY	FALSE

SEC_RETURN_SERVER_RELEASE_BANNER

Controls the display of the product version information, such as the release number, in a client connection. An intruder could use the database release number to find information about security vulnerabilities that may be present in the database software. You can enable or disable the detailed product version display by setting this parameter.

O7_DICTIONARY_ACCESSIBILITY

Set O7_DICTIONARY_ACCESSIBILITY to False to prevent users with the 'Select ANY' privilege from reading data dictionary tables. False is the default for the 12c database.

Parameters Used to Secure User Accounts

Parameter	Default Setting
SEC_CASE_SENSITIVE_LOGON	TRUE
SEC_MAX_FAILED_LOGIN_ATTEMPTS	No default setting
FAILED_LOGIN_ATTEMPTS	10
PASSWORD_GRACE_TIME	7
PASSWORD_LIFE_TIME	180
PASSWORD_LOCK_TIME	1
PASSWORD_REUSE_MAX	UNLIMITED
PASSWORD_REUSE_TIME	UNLIMITED

SEC_CASE_SENSITIVE_LOGON

Controls case sensitivity in passwords. TRUE enables case sensitivity; FALSE disables it.

SEC_MAX_FAILED_LOGIN_ATTEMPTS

Sets the maximum number of times a user is allowed to fail when connecting to an OCI application.

FAILED_LOGIN_ATTEMPTS

Sets the maximum times a user login is allowed to fail before locking the account.

Note: You also can set limits on the number of times an unauthorised user (possibly an intruder) attempts to log in to OCI applications by using the SEC_MAX_FAILED_LOGIN_ATTEMPTS initialization parameter.

PASSWORD_GRACE_TIME

Sets the number of days that a user has to change his or her password before it expires.

PASSWORD_LIFE_TIME

Sets the number of days the user can use his or her current password.

PASSWORD_LOCK_TIME

Sets the number of days an account will be locked after the specified number of consecutive failed login attempts.

PASSWORD_REUSE_MAX

Specifies the number of password changes required before the current password can be reused.

PASSWORD_REUSE_TIME

Specifies the number of days before which a password cannot be reused.

Initialization Parameters Used for Network Security

Initialization Parameter	Default Setting
OS_AUTHENT_PREFIX	OPS$
REMOTE_LISTENER	No default setting
REMOTE_OS_AUTHENT	FALSE
REMOTE_OS_ROLES	FALSE

REMOTE_OS_ROLES

Specifies whether operating system roles are allowed for remote clients. The default value, FALSE, causes Oracle Database to identify and manage roles for remote clients

REMOTE_OS_AUTHENT

Specifies whether remote clients will be authenticated with the value of the OS_AUTHENT_PREFIX parameter.

OS_AUTHENT_PREFIX

Specifies a prefix that Oracle Database uses to identify users attempting to connect to the database. Oracle Database concatenates the value of this parameter to the beginning of the user operating system account name and password. When a user attempts a connection request, Oracle Database compares the prefixed username with user names in the database.

REMOTE_LISTENER

Specifies a network name that resolves to an address or address list of Oracle Net remote listeners (that is, listeners that are not running on the same computer as this instance). The address or address list is specified in the tnsnames.ora file or another address repository as configured for your system.

Initialization Parameters Used for Auditing

Initialization Parameter	Default Setting
AUDIT_TRAIL	DB
AUDIT_FILE_DEST	*ORACLE_BASE/admin/ORACLE_SID/adump*
	Or
	ORACLE_HOME/rdbms/audit
AUDIT_SYS_OPERATIONS	FALSE
AUDIT_SYSLOG_LEVEL	No default setting

AUDIT_TRAIL

Enables or disables auditing. "DB" enable auditing at the database level and record the information in the SYS.AUD$ table.

For a full listing of the AUDIT_TRAIL parameters and an example of setting them, see Auditing Chapter.

AUDIT_FILE_DEST

ORACLE_BASE/admin/ORACLE_SID/adump

Specifies the operating system directory into which the audit trail is written when the AUDIT_TRAIL initialization parameter is set to OS, XML, or XML, EXTENDED. Oracle

Database writes the audit records in XML format if the AUDIT_TRAIL initialization parameter is set to XML.

ORACLE_HOME/rdbms/audit

Oracle Database also writes mandatory auditing information to this location, and if the AUDIT_SYS_OPERATIONS initialization parameter is set, writes audit records for user SYS

AUDIT_SYS_OPERATIONS

Enables or disables the auditing of top-level operations directly issued by user SYS, and users connecting with SYSDBA or SYSOPER privilege. Oracle Database writes the audit records to the audit trail of the operating system. If you set the AUDIT_TRAIL initialization parameter to XML or XML, EXTENDED, it writes the audit records in XML format.

On UNIX systems, if you have also set the AUDIT_SYSLOG_LEVEL parameter, then it overrides the AUDIT_TRAIL parameter, which writes the SYS audit records to the system audit log using the SYSLOG utility.

AUDIT_SYSLOG_LEVEL

On UNIX systems, writes the SYS and standard OS audit records to the system audit log using the SYSLOG utility

CONCLUSION

All these recommended parameters will help to protect the database and communication, so whenever you setup a database, you must ensure the parameters are with the correct value as per the oracle recommendation, otherwise that will create a security issue. All these parameters might change in the future releases of Oracle, so please refer the Oracle document always.

VIRTUAL PRIVATE DATABASE

Introduction

Oracle's Virtual Private Database is a feature that combines fine-grained access control with secure application context to provide a row-level security. Virtual Private Databases (VPD) allow multiple users to access a single schema while preventing them from accessing data that is not relevant to them. Although this type of access can be controlled by the application, access via other methods (SQL*Plus) would leave the data open to abuse. VPD uses Fine-Grained Access Control to limit which data is visible to specific users and Virtual1 Private Database is available in Oracle Database Enterprise Edition and it does not require additional licence costs.

VPD Setup contains the following steps:

1. Sample Schema and data creation
2. Application Context creation
3. Logon trigger creation
4. Security Policy creation
5. Apply the Security Policy
6. Test VPD

The main components of the VPD are the application context and the security policy. Both the application context and the security policy are associated with PL/SQL packages. Packages are collections of procedures and/or functions. Functions are executable statements that accept input parameters, process them and return values to the procedure which called the function. Packages are stored in the database. Therefore, packages are collections of executable code stored in the database. The application context captures the pertinent characteristics of the user. The security policy contains instructions for writing 'where' clauses for specific tables. The security policy refers to the application context to

[1] https://www.giac.org/paper/gsec/2692/oracles-virtual-private-database/102024

build the 'where' clauses based on the characteristics of the user. We will execute the VPD setup step and will understand this concept.

VIRTUAL PRIVATE DATABASE SETUP

1. Sample Schema and data creation

In this step, we are creating sample schemas and sample tables

OWNER SCHEMA AND USERSCHEMA CREATION

```
CONNECT / AS SYSDBA;

CREATE USER VPDOWNER IDENTIFIED BY VPDOWNER

DEFAULT TABLESPACE users TEMPORARY TABLESPACE temp;

GRANT connect, resource TO VPDOWNER;

CREATE USER RAM IDENTIFIED BY VPDUSER1

DEFAULT TABLESPACE users TEMPORARY TABLESPACE temp;

GRANT connect, resource TO RAM;

CREATE USER RAJ IDENTIFIED BY VPDUSER2

DEFAULT TABLESPACE users TEMPORARY TABLESPACE temp;

GRANT connect, resource TO RAJ;

GRANT EXECUTE ON DBMS_RLS TO PUBLIC;
```

CREATING SAMPLE TABLE CREATION

```
CONN VPDOWNER/VPDOWNER@VPDOWNER

CREATE TABLE users

(id NUMBER(10) NOT NULL,

ouser VARCHAR2(30) NOT NULL,

first_name VARCHAR2(50) NOT NULL,

last_name VARCHAR2(50) NOT NULL);
```

```
CREATE TABLE user_data

(column1 VARCHAR2(50) NOT NULL,

user_id NUMBER(10) NOT NULL);

insert into user_data values (1111,'ram');

insert into user_data values (2222,'raj');

INSERT INTO users VALUES (1111,'adsp','User','One');

INSERT INTO users VALUES (2222,'adsp','User','Two');

INSERT INTO users VALUES (1111,'adsp','User','One');

INSERT INTO users VALUES (2222,'ocks','User','Two');

COMMIT;

GRANT SELECT, INSERT ON user TO RAM, RAJ;

GRANT SELECT, INSERT ON user_data TO RAM, RAJ;
```

2. Application Context creation

What is Application Context?

The application context is the component that specifies the characteristics of the user who are used in determining what rows the user should be allowed to access. There are two database object types involved: the 'context' and a 'package', which implements the context. Let us deconstruct some more formal definitions.

"Application contexts are secure namespaces that identify the current values for the application-specific attributes you designate."

A namespace is an area in which no two objects can have the same name. What this means is that "context names are unique across an entire database, to ensure that contexts can't be duplicated or spoofed by individual users, either inadvertently or maliciously". When a user tries to reference an object name that is not qualified with an owner name, Oracle assumes that the user owns the object. If contexts followed this convention, a user with the 'create any context' system privilege would be able to substitute a private context to elevate his / her privileges. Instead, all application contexts are owned by the user 'SYS', regardless of which user executes the 'create any context' statement.

The 'create any context' statement simply associates the context name with a package. It is the package that specifies the attributes that will be used to determine whether the user should have access to a given row and populates the variables for the user's session.

The package is a PL/SQL program which defines and initialises variables which describe the user. The information would be selected from the application's tables. The package would include a 'dbms_session.set_context' statement that essentially commits the variable values to memory.

Information could also be selected from the data that the system collects about the user session, including the name of the user logged in and the IP address. USERENV is "a special context namespace, the user environment, which is automatically created by Oracle". (Just to confuse matters, USERENV is also a function.) When USERENV is used as a context namespace, the function SYS_CONTEXT is used to retrieve information from it. "An application context functions as a cache for repeatedly used application-oriented information." That is, once the context is initialised for the user session, the variables describing the user remain in memory for reference by the security policy throughout the session, or until the context is explicitly refreshed.

Recapping the package that implements the application context gathers information about the user either from application tables or from the system's session data and holds that information in memory.

Most articles on this topic recommend that the application context be set when the user connects to the database by means of a database trigger. If the context is set after connection by the application code, it may be possible to bypass the security policy restrictions, depending on how the policy is written. Let us create the application context.

```
APPLICATION CONTEXT CREATION:

CONNECT / AS SYSDBA;
```

```
GRANT create any context, create public synonym TO VPDOWNER;

CREATING THE APPLICATION CONTEXT:

CONNECT VPDOWNER/VPDOWNER@VPDOWNER;

CREATE CONTEXT VPDOWNER USING VPDOWNER.context_package;
```

CONTEXT PACKAGE CREATION

```
CREATE OR REPLACE PACKAGE context_package AS

PROCEDURE set_context;

END;

/
```

CONTEXT PACKAGE BODY CREATION

```
CREATE OR REPLACE PACKAGE BODY context_package IS

PROCEDURE set_context IS

v_ouser VARCHAR2(30);

v_id NUMBER;

BEGIN

DBMS_SESSION.set_context('VPDOWNER','SETUP','TRUE');

v_ouser := SYS_CONTEXT('USERENV','SESSION_USER');

BEGIN

SELECT id

INTO v_id

FROM users

WHERE ouser = v_ouser;

DBMS_SESSION.set_context('VPDOWNER','USER_ID', v_id);

EXCEPTION
```

```
WHEN NO_DATA_FOUND THEN

DBMS_SESSION.set_context('VPDOWNER','USER_ID', 0);

END;

DBMS_SESSION.set_context('VPDOWNER','SETUP','FALSE');

END set_context;

END context_package;

/
```

GRANT ACCESS AND SYNONYM CREATION

```
GRANT EXECUTE ON VPDOWNER.context_package TO PUBLIC;

CREATE PUBLIC SYNONYM context_package FOR
VPDOWNER.context_package;
```

3. LOGIN TRIGGER CREATION

TRIGGER CREATION

```
CONNECT / AS SYSDBA;

CREATE OR REPLACE TRIGGER VPDOWNER.set_security_context

AFTER LOGON ON DATABASE

BEGIN

VPDOWNER.context_package.set_context;

END;

/
```

4. SECURITY POLICY CREATION

What is Security Policy?

The security policy is the component that builds the dynamic 'where' clauses when a SQL or PL/SQL statement is executed against a table. There are two parts involved: the 'policy' and a 'package' which implements the policy. The security policy package refers to the application context when building the 'where' clauses. Again, let us start with some more formal definitions.

The policy is a named association between a schema and object and the function that builds the 'where' clause for that object. The policy also specifies which types of statements (SELECT, INSERT, UPDATE and DELETE) are governed by the policy. If a policy exists for a given table, the database knows that it has to use the function to modify the 'where' clause of any statement executed against the table. The policy is technically not a database object, but policies are tracked in the DBA_POLICIES table in the data dictionary.

The security policy package is a PL/SQL program that contains the procedures and functions that build the modified 'where' clauses. This is called "dynamic query modification" "(A) user directly or indirectly accessing a table … with an associated security policy causes the server to dynamically modify the statement based on a "WHERE" condition (known as a predicate) returned by a function which implements the security policy".

The security policy package often begins with a procedure that initialises variables used in determining what the user should have access to. This procedure may use the 'SYS_CONTEXT' function to obtain values from the user's application context.

However, the functions that build the predicate are the heart of the security policy package. Suppose we want to restrict employees from viewing their own personal data for verification purposes, but need to allow employees in Human Resources to view all personal data. The generic SQL statement would read:

Select home_address from emp_personal_data_table where [predicate}

For most employees, the predicate might read 'emp_userid = userid'. This would allow an employee to view his / her own home address.

For an employee working in the Human Resources, the predicate might read '1 = 1'. This would allow the HR employee to see all addresses because the condition is always true.

Obviously, real-world functions would contain much more complex 'if' statements, depending on the complexity of the business rules. Good programming practices dictate that the function should in some way account for users who do not meet any of the conditions in the 'if' statement. Assumptions have always been dangerous in computer code, and the security policies are no exception. The more explicit the conditions in the policy, the more legible and robust the policy will be. Let us examine the security policy with the below step.

```
CONNECT VPDOWNER/VPDOWNER@VPDOWNER;
```

--SECURITY POLICY PACKAGE CREATION

```
CREATE OR REPLACE PACKAGE security_package AS

FUNCTION user_data_insert_security(owner VARCHAR2, objname VARCHAR2)

RETURN VARCHAR2;

FUNCTION user_data_select_security(owner VARCHAR2, objname VARCHAR2)

RETURN VARCHAR2;

END security_package;

/
```

-- SECURITY PACKAGE BODY CREATION

```
CREATE OR REPLACE PACKAGE BODY Security_Package IS

FUNCTION user_data_select_security(owner VARCHAR2, objname VARCHAR2)
RETURN VARCHAR2 IS

predicate VARCHAR2(2000);

BEGIN

predicate := '1=2';

IF (SYS_CONTEXT('USERENV','SESSION_USER') = 'VPDOWNER') THEN

predicate := NULL;

ELSE
```

165

```
predicate := 'USER_ID = SYS_CONTEXT("VPDOWNER","USER_ID")';

END IF;

RETURN predicate;

END user_data_select_security;

FUNCTION  user_data_insert_security(owner  VARCHAR2,  objname  VARCHAR2)
RETURN VARCHAR2 IS

predicate VARCHAR2(2000);

BEGIN

predicate := '1=2';

IF (SYS_CONTEXT('USERENV','SESSION_USER') = 'VPDOWNER') THEN

predicate := NULL;

ELSE

predicate := 'USER_ID = SYS_CONTEXT("VPDOWNER","USER_ID")';

END IF;

RETURN Predicate;

END user_data_insert_security;

END security_package;

/
```

--GRANT ACCESS AND SYNONYM CREATION

```
GRANT EXECUTE ON VPDOWNER.security_package TO PUBLIC;

CREATE PUBLIC SYNONYM security_package FOR VPDOWNER.security_package;
```

5. APPLY INTO VPD

The DBMS_RlS package is used to apply the security policy and it is implemented by security_package to the relevant tables.

```
BEGIN

DBMS_RLS.add_policy('VPDOWNER', 'USER_DATA', 'USER_DATA_INSERT_POLICY',

'VPDOWNER', 'SECURITY_PACKAGE.USER_DATA_INSERT_SECURITY',

'INSERT', TRUE);

DBMS_RLS.add_policy('VPDOWNER', 'USER_DATA', 'USER_DATA_SELECT_POLICY',

'VPDOWNER', 'SECURITY_PACKAGE.USER_DATA_SELECT_SECURITY',

'SELECT');

END;

/
```

6. TEST VPD

We have completed the VPD setup. Now let us test the VPD and see how the VPD work.

```
CONNECT VPDOWNER/VPDOWNER

SELECT * FROM VPDOWNER.users;

ID    OUSER

----  ------

1111   ADSP   USER       ONE

2222   ADSP   USER       TWO

1111   ADSP   USER       ONE

2222   OCKS   USER       TWO

4 row selected

CONNECT RAJ/VPDUSER1

SELECT * FROM VPDOWNER.users;

ID    OUSER FIRST_NAME  LAST_NAME

----  ------      ----------- ----------
```

```
2222   ADSP    USER        TWO

2222   OCKS    USER        TWO

2 row selected
CONNECT RAM/VPDUSER1
SELECT * FROM VPDOWNER.users;
ID    OUSER FIRST_NAME  LAST_NAME
----  ------      ----------- ----------
1111   ADSP    USER        ONE

1111   ADSP    USER        ONE

2 row selected
Insert into vpdowner.users values(1111,'segs','user','five');
1 row inserted
commit;
SELECT * FROM VPDOWNER.users;
ID    OUSER FIRST_NAME  LAST_NAME
----  ------      ----------- ----------
1111   ADSP    USER        ONE

1111   ADSP    USER        ONE

1111   SEGS    USER        FIVE

2 row selected
CONNECT RAVI/VPDTEST
SELECT * FROM VPDOWNER.users;
no row selected
```

Result and Discussion

As you can see the above result Raj user and Ram user issued the query without any WHERE condition but they got the result only their data only no other data presented to both of the users. How it works—here VPD comes into play and create the dynamic WHERE condition against the query, so users are restricted to see only their data. When we are dealing with insert though the user we have archived only the row which user already saw plus the inserted row. If the access is not authorised you will receive "ORA-28115". So no way to escape from the VPD and VPD is directly interacting with the kernel so there's no way to bypass this security. One thing in the data masking chapter is we have seen how to mask the data but if we implement the data masking when the user tries to fetch the record, it will fetch all the record but in VPD that kind of action is not possible. Therefore, you have to decide what kind of requirement you to have in your environment first analyse and identify the requirement and decide.

Conclusion

This kind of restriction is very important because some of the ad hoc queries are not triggered using application and the users are using a different tool. In that case, users are not restricted and they can access all the data. Therefore, the VPD help us to protect this kind of issue. So you should consider implementing this feature because no additional licence is required and it comes along with Enterprise edition; it also has good features to help to restrict the action.

CONFIGURING NETWORK DATA ENCRYPTION AND INTEGRITY FOR ORACLE SERVERS AND CLIENTS

You can configure native Oracle Net Services data encryption and data integrity for both servers and clients.

- ☐ Introduction
- ☐ Oracle Database Native Network Encryption Data Integrity
- ☐ Data Integrity Algorithms Support

169

☐ Configuration of Data Encryption and Integrity
☐ Conclusion

Introduction

Oracle Database enables you to encrypt data that is sent over a network. Oracle Database supports the following algorithms to support encryption and integrity.

- AES
- ARIA
- GOST
- SEED
- Triple-DES Support

AES

Oracle Database supports the Federal Information Processing Standard (FIPS) encryption algorithm, AES. AES can be used by all U.S. government organizations and businesses to protect sensitive data over a network. This encryption algorithm defines three standard key lengths, which are 128-bit, 192-bit, and 256-bit. All versions operate in outer Cipher Block Chaining (CBC) mode.

ARIA

Oracle Database supports the Academia, Research Institute, and Agency (ARIA) algorithm. This algorithm acknowledges the cooperative efforts of Korean researchers in designing the algorithm. ARIA defines three standard key lengths, which are 128-bit, 192-bit, and 256-bit. All versions operate in outer cipher CBC mode.

GOST

Oracle Database supports the GOsudarstvennyy STandart (GOST) algorithm. The GOST algorithm was created by the Euro-Asian Council for Standardization, Metrology and Certification (EACS). GOST defines a key size of 256-bits. In Oracle Database, outer CBC mode is used.

SEED

Oracle Database supports the Korea Information Security Agency (KISA) encryption algorithm, SEED.

SEED defines a key size of 128-bits. There are extensions to the standard that defines additional key sizes of 192- and 256-bits, but Oracle Database does not support these extensions. In the Oracle Database, SEED operates in outer CBC mode.

Triple-DES Support

Oracle Database supports Triple-DES encryption (3DES), which encrypts message data with three passes of the DES algorithm. 3DES is available in two-key and three-key versions, with effective key lengths of 112- bits and 168-bits, respectively. Both versions operate in outer CBC mode.

Oracle Database Native Network Encryption Data Integrity

Encrypting network data provides data privacy so that unauthorised parties cannot view plaintext data as it passes over the network. Oracle Database also provides protection against two forms of active attacks.

Type of attack:

☐ Data modification attack
☐ Replay attack

Data Integrity Algorithms Support

A keyed, sequenced implementation of the Message Digest 5 (MD5) algorithm or the Secure Hash Algorithm (SHA-1 and SHA-2) protect against these attacks. Both of these hash algorithms create a checksum that changes if the data is altered in any way. This protection operates independently from the encryption process so you can enable data integrity with or without enabling encryption.

You can use Oracle Net Manager to configure network integrity on both the client and the server.

Configuring Encryption and Integrity Parameters Using Oracle Net Manager

Configuring Encryption on the Client and the Server Use Oracle Net Manager to configure encryption on the client and on the server. Configuring Integrity on the Client and the Server You can use Oracle Net Manager to configure network integrity on both the client and the server.

Configuring Encryption on the Client and the Server

Use Oracle Net Manager to configure encryption on the client and on the server.

1. Start Oracle Net Manager.

    (UNIX) From $ORACLE_HOME/bin, enter the following command at the

    command line:

    netmgr

2. Expand Oracle Net Configuration, and from Local, select Profile.
3. From the Naming list, select Network Security.

    The Network Security tabbed window appears.

4. Select the Encryption tab.

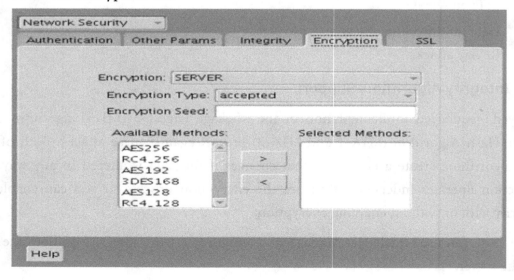

5. Select CLIENT or SERVER option from the Encryption box.

6. From the Encryption Type list, select one of the following:

    ☐ REQUESTED

    ☐ REQUIRED

    ☐ ACCEPTED

    ☐ REJECTED

7. (Optional) In the Encryption Seed field, enter between 10 and 70 random characters. The encryption seed for the client should not be the same as that for the server.

8. Select an encryption algorithm in the Available Methods list. Move it to the selected Methods list by choosing the right arrow (>). Repeat for each additional method you want to use.

9. Select File, Save Network Configuration. The sqlnet.ora file is updated.

10. Repeat this procedure to configure encryption on the other system. The sqlnet.ora file on the two systems should contain the following entries:

    ☐ On the server:

SQLNET.ENCRYPTION_SERVER = [accepted | rejected | requested | required]

SQLNET.ENCRYPTION_TYPES_SERVER = (valid_encryption_algorithm

[,valid_encryption_algorithm])

    ☐ On the client:

SQLNET.ENCRYPTION_CLIENT = [accepted | rejected | requested | required]

SQLNET.ENCRYPTION_TYPES_CLIENT = (valid_encryption_algorithm

[,valid_encryption_algorithm])

Valid Encryption Algorithms

Algorithm Name	Legal Value
AES 256-bit key	AES256
AES 192-bit key	AES192
AES 128-bit key	AES128

Client Setting	Server Setting	Encryption and Data Negotiation
REJECTED	REJECTED	OFF
ACCEPTED	REJECTED	OFF
REQUESTED	REJECTED	OFF
REQUIRED	REJECTED	Connection fails
REJECTED	ACCEPTED	OFF
ACCEPTED	ACCEPTED	OFF1
REQUESTED	ACCEPTED	ON
REQUIRED	ACCEPTED	ON
REJECTED	REQUESTED	OFF
ACCEPTED	REQUESTED	ON
REQUESTED	REQUESTED	ON
REQUIRED	REQUESTED	ON
REJECTED	REQUIRED	Connection fails
ACCEPTED	REQUIRED	ON
REQUESTED	REQUIRED	ON
REQUIRED	REQUIRED	ON

Configuring Integrity on the Client and the Server

1. Start Oracle Net Manager.

    ☐ (UNIX) From $ORACLE_HOME/bin, enter the following command at the command line:

    netmgr

2. Expand Oracle Net Configuration, and from Local, select Profile.

174

3. From the Naming list, select Network Security.

   The Network Security tabbed window appears.

4. Select the Integrity tab.

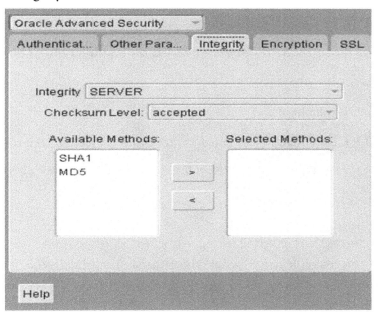

5. Depending upon which system you are configuring, select the Server or Client from the Integrity box.

6. From the Checksum Level list, select one of the following Checksum Level values:
   - REQUESTED
   - REQUIRED
   - ACCEPTED
   - REJECTED

7. Select an integrity algorithm in the Available Methods list. Move it to the Selected Methods list by choosing the right arrow (>). Repeat for each additional method you want to use.

8. Select File, Save Network Configuration.

   The sqlnet.ora file is updated.

9. Repeat this procedure to configure integrity on the other system.

The sqlnet.ora file on the two systems should contain the following entries:

☐ On the server:

SQLNET.CRYPTO_CHECKSUM_SERVER = [accepted | rejected | requested | required]

SQLNET.CRYPTO_CHECKSUM_TYPES_SERVER = (valid_crypto_checksum_algorithm

[,valid_crypto_checksum_algorithm])

☐ On the client:

SQLNET.CRYPTO_CHECKSUM_CLIENT = [accepted | rejected | requested | required]

SQLNET.CRYPTO_CHECKSUM_TYPES_CLIENT = (valid_crypto_checksum_algorithm

[,valid_crypto_checksum_algorithm])

Conclusion

In this chapter, you have learned what algorithms used in Oracle Database for data encryption and integrity and how to enable these algorithms configurations in oracle server and client level.

CONFIGURING THE THIN JDBC CLIENT NETWORK

Oracle Database native network encryption and strong authentication enables thin JDBC clients to securely connect to Oracle databases

☐ Introduction
☐ JDBC Support
☐ JDBC Features
☐ Implementation Overview
☐ Obfuscation of the Java Cryptography Code
☐ Configuration Parameters for the Thin JDBC Network Implementation
☐ Conclusion

Introduction

Java implementation of native network encryption and strong authentication in Oracle Database that provides network authentication, encryption and integrity protection for Thin JDBC clients that must communicate with Oracle Databases that have Oracle Database native network encryption and strong authentication configured.

JDBC Support

JDBC, an industry-standard Java interface, is a Java standard for connecting to a relational database from a Java program. Sun Microsystems defined the JDBC standard and Oracle implements and extends the standard with its own JDBC drivers. Oracle JDBC drivers are used to create JDBC applications to communicate with Oracle databases. Oracle implements two types of JDBC drivers: Thick JDBC drivers built on top of the C-based Oracle Net client, as well as a Thin (Pure Java) JDBC driver to support downloadable applets. Oracle extensions to JDBC include the following features:

- Data access and manipulation
- LOB access and manipulation
- Oracle object type mapping
- Object reference access and manipulation
- Array access and manipulation
- Application performance enhancement

JDBC Features

The Thin JDBC driver provides security features such as strong authentication, data encryption, and data integrity checking. Oracle designed a 100 per cent Java implementation of Oracle Database native network encryption and strong authentication, encryption, and integrity algorithms, for use with thin clients.

Oracle Database provides the following features for Thin JDBC:

☐ Strong Authentication
☐ Data encryption
☐ Data integrity checking

- Secure connections from Thin JDBC clients to the Oracle RDBMS
- The ability for developers to build applets that transmit data over a secure communication channel
- Secure connections from middle-tier servers with Java Server Pages (JSP) to the Oracle RDBMS
- Secure connections from Oracle Database 12c release 1 (12.1) to older versions of Oracle databases

The Oracle JDBC Thin driver supports the Oracle Database SSL implementation and third-party authentication methods such as RADIUS and Kerberos. Thin JDBC support for authentication methods like RADIUS, Kerberos, and SSL were introduced in Oracle Database 11g release 1 (11.1).

Implementation Overview

On the server side, the negotiation of algorithms and the generation of keys function exactly the same as Oracle Database native encryption.

This feature enables backward and forward compatibility of clients and servers. On the client side, the algorithm negotiation and key generation occur in exactly the same manner as OCI clients. The client and server negotiate encryption algorithms, generate random numbers, use Diffie-Hellman to exchange session keys, and use the Oracle Password Protocol, in the same manner as the traditional Oracle Net clients. Thin JDBC contains a complete implementation of an Oracle Net client in pure Java.

Obfuscation of the Java Cryptography Code

The obfuscation of the Java cryptography code protects Java classes and methods that contain encryption and decryption capabilities with obfuscation software. Java byte code obfuscator is a process frequently used to protect intellectual property written in the form of Java programs. It mixes up Java symbols found in the code. The process leaves the original program structure intact, letting the program run correctly while changing the names of the classes, methods, and variables in order to hide the intended behaviour. Although it is possible to decompile and read non-obfuscated Java code, obfuscated Java code is sufficiently difficult to decompile to satisfy U.S. government export controls.

Configuration Parameters for the Thin JDBC Network Implementation

Parameter Name	Parameter Type	Possible Settings
CONNECTION_PROPERTY_THIN_NET_ENCRYPTION_LEVEL	String	REJECTED ACCEPTED REQUESTED REQUIRED
CONNECTION_PROPERTY_THIN_NET_ENCRYPTION_TYPES	String	AES256, AES192, AES128, 3DES168, 3DES112, DES56C, DES40C, RC4_256, RC4_128, RC4_40, RC4_56
CONNECTION_PROPERTY_THIN_NET_CHECKSUM_LEVEL	String	REJECTED ACCEPTED REQUESTED REQUIRED
CONNECTION_PROPERTY_THIN_NET_CHECKSUM_TYPES	String	MD5, SHA1
CONNECTION_PROPERTY_THIN_NET_AUTHENTICATION_SERVICES	String	RADIUS, KERBEROS, SSL

The Thin JDBC network implementation for the client provides parameters to control encryption, integrity, and the authentication service. The JDBC network implementation configuration parameters control network settings such as the level of security used between client and server connections. A properties class object containing several configuration parameters is passed to the Oracle Database native network encryption and strong authentication interface. All JDBC connection properties including the ones

179

pertaining to Oracle Database are defined as constants in the oracle.jdbc.OracleConnection interface.

The following list Thin Driver Client Parameters for Encryption and Integrity

CONNECTION_PROPERTY_THIN_NET_ENCRYPTION_LEVEL

This parameter defines the level of security that the client uses to negotiate with the server.

Syntax:

prop.setProperty(OracleConnection.CONNECTION_PROPERTY_THIN_NET_ENCRYPTION_LEVEL,*level*);

Example:

prop.setProperty(OracleConnection.CONNECTION_PROPERTY_THIN_NET_ENCRYPTION_LEVEL,"REQUIRED");

CONNECTION_PROPERTY_THIN_NET_ENCRYPTION_TYPES

This parameter defines the encryption algorithm to be used.

Syntax:

prop.setProperty(OracleConnection.CONNECTION_PROPERTY_THIN_NET_ENCRYPTION_TYPES,*algorithm*);

Example:

prop.setProperty(OracleConnection.CONNECTION_PROPERTY_THIN_NET_ENCRYPTION_TYPES, "(AES256,AES192)");

CONNECTION_PROPERTY_THIN_NET_CHECKSUM_LEVEL

This parameter defines the level of security to negotiate with the server for data integrity.

Syntax:

prop.setProperty(OracleConnection.CONNECTION_PROPERTY_THIN_NET_CHECKSUM_LEVEL,level);

Example:

prop.setProperty(OracleConnection.CONNECTION_PROPERTY_THIN_NET_CHECKS UM_LEVEL,"REQUIRED");

CONNECTION_PROPERTY_THIN_NET_CHECKSUM_TYPES

This parameter defines the data integrity algorithm to be used.

Syntax:

prop.setProperty(OracleConnection.CONNECTION_PROPERTY_THIN_NET_CHECKS UM_TYPES, algorithm);

Example:

prop.setProperty(OracleConnection.CONNECTION_PROPERTY_THIN_NET_CHECKS UM_TYPES,"(MD5, SHA1)");

CONNECTION_PROPERTY_THIN_NET_AUTHENTICATION_SERVICES

This parameter determines the authentication service to be used.

Syntax:

prop.setProperty(OracleConnection.CONNECTION_PROPERTY_THIN_NET_AUTHE NTICATION_SERVICES,authentication);

Example:

prop.setProperty(OracleConnection.CONNECTION_PROPERTY_THIN_NET_AUTHE NTICATION_SERVICES,"(RADIUS,KERBEROS, SSL)");

Example Server side setup:

In order to activate encryption and checksumming in the database you need to modify the sqlnet.ora file. For example:

```
SQLNET.ENCRYPTION_TYPES_SERVER = (AES256,AES192,AES128)
SQLNET.ENCRYPTION_SERVER = accepted
SQLNET.CRYPTO_CHECKSUM_TYPES_SERVER= (SHA1)
SQLNET.CRYPTO_CHECKSUM_SERVER = accepted
```

Example JDBC Client Code:

```
import java.sql.*;

import java.util.Properties;import oracle.jdbc.*;

import oracle.net.ano.AnoServices;

/**

* JDBC thin driver demo: new security features in 11gR1.

*

* This program attempts to connect to the database using the JDBC thin

* driver and requires the connection to be encrypted with either AES256 or AES192

* and the data integrity to be verified with SHA1.

*

*

* This output of this program is:

* Connection created! Encryption algorithm is: AES256, data integrity algorithm

* is: SHA1

*

*/

public class DemoAESAndSHA1

{

static final String USERNAME= "hr";

static final String PASSWORD= "hr";

static final String URL =
```

```
"jdbc:oracle:thin:@(DESCRIPTION=(ADDRESS=(PROTOCOL=tcp)(HOST=test.o
racle.com)

(PORT=5561))"

+"(CONNECT_DATA=(SERVICE_NAME=testdb.example.com))";

public static final void main(String[] argv)

{

DemoAESAndSHA1 demo = new DemoAESAndSHA1();

try

{

demo.run();

}catch(SQLException ex)

{

ex.printStackTrace();

}

}

void run() throws SQLException

{

OracleDriver dr = new OracleDriver();

Properties prop = new Properties();

// We require the connection to be encrypted with either AES256 or
AES192.

// If the database doesn't accept such a security level, then the
connection

// attempt will fail.
```

```
prop.setProperty(OracleConnection.CONNECTION_PROPERTY_THIN_NET_ENCR
YPTION_LEVEL,AnoServices.ANO_REQUIRED);

prop.setProperty(OracleConnection.CONNECTION_PROPERTY_THIN_NET_ENCR
YPTION_TYPES, "( " +AnoServices.ENCRYPTION_AES256 + ","
+AnoServices.ENCRYPTION_AES192 + ")");

// We also require the use of the SHA1 algorithm for data integrity
checking.

prop.setProperty(OracleConnection.CONNECTION_PROPERTY_THIN_NET_CHEC
KSUM_LEVEL,AnoServices.ANO_REQUIRED);

prop.setProperty(OracleConnection.CONNECTION_PROPERTY_THIN_NET_CHEC
KSUM_TYPES, "( " +

AnoServices.CHECKSUM_SHA1 + " )");

prop.setProperty("user",DemoAESAndSHA1.USERNAME);

prop.setProperty("password",DemoAESAndSHA1.PASSWORD);

OracleConnection oraConn =

(OracleConnection)dr.connect(DemoAESAndSHA1.URL,prop);

System.out.println("Connection created! Encryption algorithm is:

"+oraConn.getEncryptionAlgorithmName() +", data integrity algorithm
is:

"+oraConn.getDataIntegrityAlgorithmName());

oraConn.close();

}

}
```

Conclusion

In this chapter you have learned how to enable security for JDBC Connection and what are the parameter available to achieve that and so on.

CONFIGURING RADIUS AUTHENTICATION

RADIUS is a client/server security protocol widely used to enable remote authentication and access.

- ☐ Introduction
- ☐ RADIUS Components
- ☐ RADIUS Authentication Modes
- ☐ Enabling RADIUS Authentication, Authorization, and Accounting
- ☐ Using RADIUS to Log in to a Database
- ☐ RSA ACE/Server Configuration Checklist
- ☐ Conclusion

Introduction

RADIUS is the trusted third-party authentication service provider. In the Oracle Database network, you can use the RADIUS authentication method to protect from the network threats. When you install the RADIUS protocol, you will get the RADIUS standard, which includes token cards and smart cards. Oracle Database uses RADIUS in a client/server network environment. Moreover, when you use RADIUS, you can change the authentication method without modifying either the Oracle client or the Oracle Database server. From an end-user's perspective, the entire authentication process is transparent. When the user tries to access an Oracle Database server, the Oracle Database server, acting as the RADIUS client, notifies the RADIUS server. In addition, the RADIUS server does the following action:

- ☐ It will look up the user's security information
- ☐ Then Identified information between the appropriate authentication server or servers and the Oracle Database server
- ☐ Once user detail correct it grants the user access to the Oracle Database server
- ☐ After the connection gets established, it will log session information, including when, how often, and for how long the user was connected to the Oracle Database server

Note:

Through database links, Oracle Database does not support RADIUS authentication.

RADIUS in an Oracle Environment

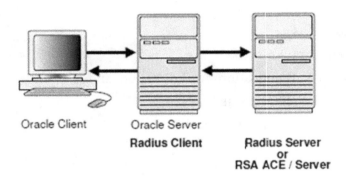

When the new connection request arise then the Oracle Database server acts as the RADIUS client, passing information between the Oracle client and the RADIUS server. Similarly, the RADIUS server passes information between the Oracle Database server and the appropriate authentication servers.

A RADIUS server vendor is often the authentication server vendor as well. In this case, authentication can be processed on the RADIUS server. For example, the RSA ACE/ Server is both a RADIUS server and an authentication server. It thus authenticates the user's passcode.

RADIUS Components

RADIUS has a set of authentication components that enable you to manage configuration settings.

RADIUS Authentication Components

Component	Stored Information
Oracle client	Configuration setting for communicating through RADIUS
Oracle Database server/ RADIUS client	Configuration settings for passing information between the Oracle client and the RADIUS server. The secret key file
RADIUS server	Authentication and authorization information for all users. Each client's name or IP address. Each client's shared secret. Unlimited number of menu files enabling users already authenticated to select different login options without reconnecting
Authentication server or servers	User authentication information such as passcodes and PINs, depending on the authentication method in use. Note: The RADIUS server can also be the authentication server

Note: The RADIUS server can also be the authentication server.

RADIUS Authentication Modes

User authentication can take place either through two modes.

- ☐ Synchronous Authentication Mode
- ☐ Challenge-Response (Asynchronous) Authentication Mode

Synchronous Authentication Mode

In the synchronous mode, RADIUS lets you use various authentication methods, including passwords and SecurID token cards.

- ☐ Sequence for Synchronous Authentication Mode

The sequence of synchronous authentication mode is comprised of six steps.

☐ Example: Synchronous Authentication with SecurID Token Cards

With SecurID authentication, each user has a token card that displays a dynamic number that changes every sixty seconds.

Sequence for Synchronous Authentication Mode

The sequence of synchronous authentication mode is comprised of six steps.

Synchronous Authentication Sequence

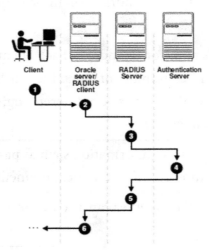

The following steps describe the synchronous authentication sequence:

1. A user logs in by entering a connect string, passcode, or other value. The client system passes this data to the Oracle Database server.
2. The Oracle Database server, acting as the RADIUS client, passes the data from the Oracle client to the RADIUS server.
3. The RADIUS server passes the data to the appropriate authentication server, such as Smart Card or SecurID ACE for validation.
4. The authentication server sends either an Access Accept or an Access Reject message back to the RADIUS server.

5. .The RADIUS server passes this response to the Oracle Database server/RADIUS client.

6. The Oracle Database server/RADIUS client passes the response back to the Oracle client.

Example: Synchronous Authentication with SecurID Token Cards

With SecurID authentication, each user has a token card that displays a dynamic number that changes every sixty seconds. To gain access to the Oracle Database server/RADIUS client, the user enters a valid passcode that includes both a personal identification number (PIN) and the dynamic number currently displayed on the user's SecurID card. The Oracle Database server passes this authentication information from the Oracle client to the RADIUS server, which in this case is the authentication server for validation. Once the authentication server (RSA ACE/Server) validates the user, it sends an *accept* packet to the Oracle Database server, which, in turn, passes it to the Oracle client. The user is now authenticated and able to access the appropriate tables and applications.

Challenge-Response (Asynchronous) Authentication Mode

When the system uses the asynchronous mode, the user does not need to enter a user name and password at the SQL*Plus CONNECT string.

- Sequence for Challenge-Response (Asynchronous) Authentication Mode
- The sequence for challenge-response (asynchronous) authentication mode is comprised of 12 steps.
- Example: Asynchronous Authentication with Smart Cards
- With smart card authentication, the user logs in by inserting the smart card into a smart card reader that reads the smart card.
- Example: Asynchronous Authentication with ActivCard Tokens
- One particular ActivCard token is a hand-held device with a keypad and which, displays a dynamic password.

Sequence for Challenge-Response (Asynchronous) Authentication Mode

The sequence for challenge-response (asynchronous) authentication mode is comprised of 12 steps.

The following steps describe the asynchronous authentication sequence:

1. A user initiates a connection to an Oracle Database server. The client system passes the data to the Oracle Database server.

2. The Oracle Database server, acting as the RADIUS client, passes the data from the Oracle client to the RADIUS server.

3. The RADIUS server passes the data to the appropriate authentication server, such as a Smart Card, SecurID ACE, or token card server.

4. The authentication server sends a challenge, such as a random number, to the RADIUS server.

5. The RADIUS server passes the challenge to the Oracle Database server/RADIUS client.

6. The Oracle Database server/RADIUS client, in turn, passes it to the Oracle client. A graphical user interface presents the challenge to the user.

7. The user provides a response to the challenge. To formulate a response, the user can, for example, enter the received challenge into the token card. The token card provides a dynamic password that is entered into the graphical user interface. The Oracle client passes the user's response to the Oracle Database server/RADIUS client.

8. The Oracle Database server/RADIUS client sends the user's response to the RADIUS server.

9. The RADIUS server passes the user's response to the appropriate authentication server for validation.

10. The authentication server sends either an Access Accept or an Access Reject message back to the RADIUS server.

11. The RADIUS server passes the response to the Oracle Database server/RADIUS client.

12. The Oracle Database server/RADIUS client passes the response to the Oracle client.

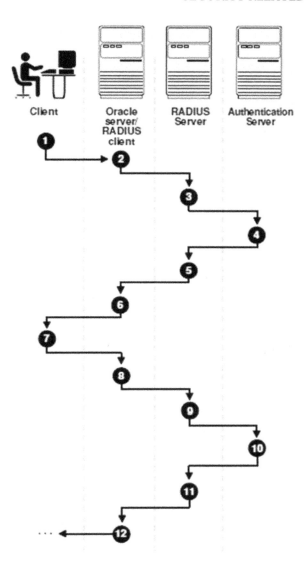

Example: Asynchronous Authentication with Smart Cards

With smart card authentication, the user logs in by inserting the smart card into a smart card reader that reads the smart card.

The smart card is a plastic card, like a credit card, with an embedded integrated circuit for storing information.

The Oracle client sends the login information contained in the smart card to the authentication server by way of the Oracle Database server/RADIUS client and the RADIUS server. The authentication server sends back a challenge to the Oracle client, by way of the RADIUS server and the Oracle Database server, prompting the user for authentication information. The information could be, for example, a PIN as well as additional authentication information contained on the smart card.

The Oracle client sends the user's response to the authentication server by way of the Oracle Database server and the RADIUS server. If the user has entered a valid number, the authentication server sends an *accept* packet back to the Oracle client by way of the RADIUS server and the Oracle Database server. The user is now authenticated and authorised to access the appropriate tables and applications. If the user has entered incorrect information, the authentication server sends back a message rejecting user's access.

Example: Asynchronous Authentication with ActivCard Tokens

One particular ActivCard token is a hand-held device with a keypad and which displays a dynamic password.

When the user seeks access to an Oracle Database server by entering a password, the information is passed to the appropriate authentication server by way of the Oracle Database server/RADIUS client and the RADIUS server. The authentication server sends back a challenge to the client, by way of the RADIUS server and the Oracle Database server. The user types that challenge into the token, and the token displays a number for the user to send in response.

The Oracle client then sends the user's response to the authentication server by way of the Oracle Database server and the RADIUS server. If the user has typed a valid number, the authentication server sends an *accept* packet back to the Oracle client by way of the RADIUS server and the Oracle Database server. The user is now authenticated and authorised to access the appropriate tables and applications. If the user has entered an incorrect response, the authentication server sends back a message rejecting the user's access.

Enabling RADIUS Authentication, Authorization, and Accounting

To enable RADIUS authentication, authorization, and accounting, you can use Oracle Net Manager.

Step 1: Configure RADIUS Authentication

To configure RADIUS authentication, you must first configure it on the Oracle client, then the server. Afterwards, you can configure additional RADIUS features.

Step 2: Create a User and Grant Access

After you complete the RADIUS authentication, you must create an Oracle Database user who for the RADIUS configuration.

Step 3: Configure External RADIUS Authorization (Optional)

You must configure the Oracle server, the Oracle client, and the RADIUS server to RADIUS users who must connect to an Oracle Database.

Step 4: Configure RADIUS Accounting

RADIUS accounting logs information about access to the Oracle Database server and stores it in a file on the RADIUS accounting server.

Step 5: Add the RADIUS Client Name to the RADIUS Server Database

The RADIUS server that you select must comply with RADIUS standards.

Step 6: Configure the Authentication Server for Use with RADIUS

After you add the RADIUS client name to the RADIUS server database, you can configure the authentication server to use the RADIUS.

Step 7: Configure the RADIUS Server for Use with the Authentication Server

After you configure the authentication server for use with RADIUS, you can configure the RADIUS server to use the authentication server.

Step 8: Configure Mapping Roles

If the RADIUS server supports vendor type attributes, then you can manage roles by storing them in the RADIUS server.

Using RADIUS to Log in to a Database

You can use RADIUS to log into a database by using either synchronous authentication mode or challenge-response mode.

Start SQL*Plus and use one of the following ways to log in to the database:

– If you are using the synchronous authentication mode, first ensure that challenge-response mode is not turned to ON, and then enter the following

command:

CONNECT username@database_alias

Enter password: password

– If you are using the challenge-response mode, ensure that challenge-response mode is set to ON and then enter the following command:

CONNECT /@*database_alias*

Note: The challenge-response mode can be configured for all login cases.

RSA ACE/Server Configuration Checklist

If you are using an RSA ACE/Server RADIUS server, check the host agent and SecurID tokens for this server before making the initial connection.

- Ensure that the host agent in the RSA ACE/Server is set up to send a node secret. In version 5.0, this is done by leaving the SENT Node secret box unchecked. If the RSA ACE/Server fails to send a node secret to the agent, then a node verification failure message will be written to the RSA ACE/Server log.
- If you are using RSA SecurID tokens, then ensure that the token is synchronised with the RSA ACE/Server.

Conclusion

It is a good authentication method and it has features like RSA ACE/Server and smart card and the token card is nice. With this many options we can ensure no user authorised to access the database without having the proper permission. Therefore, to enable protected environment we can implement RADIUS Protocol.

CONFIGURING KERBEROS AUTHENTICATION

Kerberos is a trusted third-party authentication system that relies on shared secrets and presumes that the third-party is secure.

- ☐ Introduction
- ☐ Enabling Kerberos Authentication
- ☐ Utilities for the Kerberos Authentication Adapter
- ☐ Connecting to an Oracle Database Server Authenticated by Kerberos
- ☐ Configuring Kerberos Authentication Fallback Behaviour
- ☐ Conclusion

Introduction

Oracle network security support for Kerberos authentication and It provides the benefits of single sign-on and centralised authentication of Oracle users. Kerberos is a trusted third-party authentication system that relies on shared secrets. It presumes that the third-party is secure, and provides single sign-on capabilities, centralised password storage, database link authentication, and enhanced PC security. It does this through a Kerberos authentication server, or through Cybersafe Active Trust, a commercial Kerberos-based authentication server.

Enabling Kerberos Authentication

To enable Kerberos authentication for Oracle Database, you must first install it, and then follow a set of configuration steps.

- ☐ Step 1: Install Kerberos
- ☐ Step 2: Configure a Service Principal for an Oracle Database Server
- ☐ Step 3: Extract a Service Key Table from Kerberos
- ☐ Step 4: Install an Oracle Database Server and an Oracle Client
- ☐ Step 5: Configure Oracle Net Services and Oracle Database
- ☐ Step 6: Configure Kerberos Authentication

   ☐ Step 7: Create a Kerberos User

   ☐ Step 8: Create an Externally Authenticated Oracle User

   ☐ Step 9: Get an Initial Ticket for the Kerberos/Oracle User

Step 1: Install Kerberos

You should install Kerberos Version 5.

The source distribution for notes about building and installing Kerberos provide details. After you install Kerberos, if you are using IBM AIX on POWER systems (64-bit), You should ensure that Kerberos 5 is the preferred authentication method.

1. Install Kerberos on the system that functions as the authentication server.
2. For IBM AIX on POWER systems (64-bit), check the authentication method.

   For example:

   /usr/bin/lsauthent

   Output similar to the following may appear:

   Standard Aix

3. Configure Kerberos 5 as the preferred method.

   For example:

   /usr/bin/chauthent -k5 -std

   This command sets Kerberos 5 as the preferred authentication method (k5) and Standard AIX as the second (std).

4. To ensure that Kerberos 5 is now the preferred method, check the new configuration.

   /usr/bin/lsauthent

   Kerberos 5

   Standard Aix

Step 2: Configure a Service Principal for an Oracle Database Server

You must create a service principal for Oracle Database before the server can validate the identity of clients that authenticate themselves using Kerberos.

1. Decide on a name for the service principal, using the following format:

    kservice/kinstance@REALM

Note:

kservice - A case-sensitive string that represents the Oracle service. This can be the same as the database service name.

kinstance - Typically the fully qualified DNS name of the system on which Oracle Database is running.

REALM - The name of the Kerberos realm with which the service principal is registered. REALM must always be uppercase and is typically the DNS domain name.

The utility names in this section are executable programs. However, the Kerberos user name krbuser and the realm EXAMPLE.COM are examples only.

For example, suppose kservice is Oracle, the fully qualified name of the system on which Oracle Database is running is dbserver.example.com and the realm is EXAMPLE.COM.

The principal name then is:

oracle/dbserver.example.com@EXAMPLE.COM

2. Run kadmin.local to create the service principal. On UNIX, run this command as the root user, by using the following syntax:

    # cd /kerberos-install-directory/sbin

    # ./kadmin.local

For example, to add a principal named oracle/dbserver.example.com@EXAMPLE.COM to the list of server principals known by

Kerberos, you can enter the following:

kadmin.local:addprinc -randkey oracle/dbserver.example.com@EXAMPLE.COM

Step 3: Extract a Service Key Table from Kerberos

Next, you are ready to extract the service key table from Kerberos and copy it to the Oracle Database server/Kerberos client system.

For example, to extract a service key table for dbserver.example.com:

1. Enter the following to extract the service key table:

   kadmin.local: ktadd -k /tmp/keytab oracle/dbserver.example.com

   Entry for principal oracle/dbserver.example.com with kvno 2,

   encryption type AES-256 CTS mode with 96-bit SHA-1 HMAC added to keytab WRFILE:

   WRFILE:/tmp/keytab

   kadmin.local: exit

2. To check the service key table, enter the following command:

   oklist -k -t /tmp/keytab

3. After the service key table has been extracted, verify that the new entries are in the table in addition to the old ones.

   If they are not, or you need to add more, use kadmin.local to append to them.

   If you do not enter a realm when using ktadd, it uses the default realm of the Kerberos server. kadmin.local is connected to the Kerberos server running on the localhost.

4. If the Kerberos service key table is on the same system as the Kerberos client, you can move it. If the service key table is on a different system from the Kerberos client, you must transfer the file with a program such as FTP. If using FTP, transfer the file in binary mode.

   The following example shows how to move the service key table on a UNIX platform:

   # mv /tmp/keytab /etc/v5srvtab

The default name of the service file is /etc/v5srvtab.

5. Verify that the owner of the Oracle Database server executable can read the service key table (/etc/v5srvtab in the previous example).

To do so, set the file owner to the Oracle user, or make the file readable by the group to which Oracle belongs.

Do not make the file readable to all users. This can cause a security breach.

Step 4: Install an Oracle Database Server and an Oracle Client

After you extract a service key table from Kerberos, you are ready to install the Oracle Database server and an Oracle client.

Step 5: Configure Oracle Net Services and Oracle Database

After you install the Oracle Database server and client, you can configure Oracle Net Services on the server and client.

Step 6: Configure Kerberos Authentication

You must set the required parameters in the Oracle Database server and client sqlnet.ora files.

Note: Be aware that in a multitenant environment, the settings in the sqlnet.ora file applies to all pluggable databases (PDBs). However, this does not mean that all PDBs must authenticate with one KDC if using Kerberos; the settings in the sqlnet.ora file and Kerberos configuration files can support multiple KDCs.

- ☐ Configure Kerberos on the Client and on the Database Server
- ☐ Set the Initialization Parameters
- ☐ Set sqlnet.ora Parameters (Optional)

Configure Kerberos on the Client and on the Database Server

First, you must configure Kerberos authentication service parameters on the client and on the database server.

1. Start Oracle Net Manager.

- (UNIX) From *$ORACLE_HOME*/bin, enter the following command at the command line:
- Netmgr

2. Expand **Oracle Net Configuration**, and from **Local**, select **Profile**.
3. From the **Naming** list, select **Network Security**.
4. Select the **Authentication** tab.
5. From the Available Methods list, select **KERBEROS5**.
6. Move **KERBEROS5** to the Selected Methods list by clicking the right arrow (>).
7. Arrange the selected methods in order of use.

To do so, select a method in the Selected Methods list, then click **Promote** or **Demote** to position it in the list. For example, if you want KERBEROS5 to be the first service used, move it to the top of the list.

8. Select the **Other Params** tab.
9. From the Authentication Service list, select **KERBEROS(V5)**.
10. Type **Kerberos** into the **Service** field.

    This field defines the name of the service Oracle Database uses to obtain a Kerberos service ticket. When you provide the value for this field, the other fields are enabled.

11. Optionally enter values for the following fields:
    - ☐ Credential Cache File
    - ☐ Configuration File
    - ☐ Realm Translation File
    - ☐ Key Table
    - ☐ Clock Skew

12. From the File menu, select Save Network Configuration.

The sqlnet.ora file is updated with the following entries in addition to any optional choices that you may have made in the previous step:

SQLNET.AUTHENTICATION_SERVICES=(KERBEROS5)

SQLNET.AUTHENTICATION_KERBEROS5_SERVICE=kservice

Set the Initialization Parameters

Next, you are ready to set the OS_AUTHENT_PREFIX initialization parameter.

1. Locate the init.ora file.

By default, the init.ora file is located in the *ORACLE_HOME*/dbs directory (or the same location of the data files) on Linux and UNIX systems,

In the init.ora file, set the value of OS_AUTHENT_PREFIX to null in the init.ora initialization parameter file.

For example:

OS_AUTHENT_PREFIX=""""

Set this value to null because Kerberos user names can be long, and Oracle user names are limited to 30 characters. Setting this parameter to null overrides the default value of OPS$.

Note: You can create external database users that have Kerberos user names of more than 30 characters.

Set sqlnet.ora Parameters (Optional)

You can set optional sqlnet.ora parameters, in addition to the required parameters, for better security.

- Optionally, set the parameters listed in the following table on both the client and the Oracle Database

1. SQLNET.KERBEROS5_CC_NAME=pathname_to_credentials_cache_file|

For example:

SQLNET.KERBEROS5_CC_NAME=/usr/tmp/krbcache

2. SQLNET.KERBEROS5_CLOCKSKEW=number_of_seconds_accepted_as_network_delay

For example:

SQLNET.KERBEROS5_CLOCKSKEW=1200

3. SQLNET.KERBEROS5_CONF=pathname_to_Kerberos_configuration_file|AUTO _DISCOVER

   For example:

   SQLNET.KERBEROS5_CONF=/krb/krb.conf

   SQLNET.KERBEROS5_CONF=AUTO_DISCOVER

4. SQLNET.KERBEROS5_CONF_LOCATION=*path_to_Kerberos_configuration_dire ctory*

   For example:

   SQLNET.KERBEROS5_CONF_LOCATION=/krb

5. SQLNET.KERBEROS5_KEYTAB=*path_to_Kerberos_principal/key_table*

   For example:

   SQLNET.KERBEROS5_KEYTAB=/etc/v5srvtab

6. SQLNET.KERBEROS5_REALMS=*path_to_Kerberos_realm_translation_file*

   For example:

   SQLNET.KERBEROS5_REALMS=/krb5/krb.realms

Step 7: Create a Kerberos User

You must create the Kerberos user on the Kerberos authentication server where the administration tools are installed.

The realm must already exist.

Note: The utility names in this section are executable programs. However, the Kerberos user name krbuser and realm EXAMPLE.COM are examples only.

They can vary among systems.

☐ Run /krb5/admin/kadmin.local as root to create a new Kerberos user, such as

krbuser.

For example, to create a Kerberos user is UNIX-specific:

/krb5/admin/kadmin.local

kadmin.local: **addprinc krbuser**

Enter password for principal: "krbuser@example.com": (password does not display)

Re-enter password for principal: "krbuser@example.com": (password does not display)

kadmin.local: **exit**

Step 8: Create an Externally Authenticated Oracle User

Next, you are ready to create an externally authenticated Oracle user.

1. Log in to SQL*Plus as a user who has the CREATE USER privilege.

    sqlplus sec_admin - *Or, CONNECT sec_admin@hrpdb*

    Enter password: *password*

2. Ensure that the OS_AUTHENT_PREFIX is set to null ("").
3. Create an Oracle Database user account that corresponds to the Kerberos user. Enter the Oracle user name in uppercase and enclose it in double quotation marks.

For example:

    CREATE USER "KRBUSER@EXAMPLE.COM" IDENTIFIED EXTERNALLY;

    GRANT CREATE SESSION TO "KRBUSER@EXAMPLE.COM";

If the user's Kerberos principal name is longer than 30 characters, and up to 1024 characters, then create the user by using the following syntax:

    CREATE USER *db_user_name* IDENTIFIED EXTERNALLY AS
    '*kerberos_principal_name*';

For example:

    CREATE USER KRBUSER IDENTIFIED EXTERNALLY AS
    'KerberosUser@example.com';

Note:

The database administrator should ensure that two database users are not identified externally by the same Kerberos principal name.

Step 9: Get an Initial Ticket for the Kerberos/Oracle User

Before you can connect to the database, you must ask the KDC for an initial ticket.

☐ To request an initial ticket, run the following command on the client:

% okinit *username*

If you want to enable credentials that can be used across database links, then include the -f option and provide the Kerberos password when prompted.

% okinit -f

Password for krbuser@EXAMPLE.COM:(password does not display)

Utilities for the Kerberos Authentication Adapter

The Oracle Kerberos authentication adapter utilities are designed for an Oracle client with Oracle Kerberos authentication support installed.

- ☐ okinit Utility
- ☐ oklist Utility
- ☐ okdstry Utility
- ☐ okcreate Utility

okinit Utility

The okinit utility obtains and caches Kerberos tickets. This utility is typically used to obtain the ticket-granting ticket, using a password entered by the user to decrypt the credential from the KDC. The ticket-granting ticket is then stored in the user's credential cache.

To use the functionality , you must set the sqlnet.ora

SQLNET.KERBEROS5_CONF_MIT parameter to TRUE. (Note that SQLNET.KERBEROS5_CONF_MIT is deprecated, but is retained for backward compatibility for okinit.)

oklist Utility

The oklist utility displays the list of tickets held.

To use the functionality , you must set the sqlnet.ora SQLNET.KERBEROS5_CONF_MIT

parameter to TRUE. (Note that SQLNET.KERBEROS5_CONF_MIT is deprecated, but is retained for backward compatibility for oklist.)

okdstry Utility

The okdstry (okdestroy) utility removes credentials from the cache file.

To use the functionality that , you must set the sqlnet.ora SQLNET.KERBEROS5_CONF_MIT

parameter to TRUE. (Note that SQLNET.KERBEROS5_CONF_MIT is deprecated, but is retained for backward compatibility for okdstry.)

okcreate Utility

The okcreate utility automates the creation of keytabs from either the KDC or a service endpoint.

Connecting to an Oracle Database Server Authenticated by Kerberos

After Kerberos is configured, you can connect to an Oracle Database server without using a user name or password.

- Use the following syntax to connect to the database without using a user name or password:

  $ sqlplus /@*net_service_name*

  In this specification, *net_service_name* is an Oracle Net Services service name.

  For example:

  $ sqlplus /@oracle_dbname

Configuring Kerberos Authentication Fallback Behaviour

- ☐ Check that the sqlnet.ora file on the database server side has a service name that corresponds to a service known by Kerberos.
- ☐ Check that the clocks on all systems involved are set to times that are within a few minutes of each other or change the SQLNET.KERBEROS5_CLOCKSKEW parameter in the sqlnet.ora file.

  ➤ If you have a service ticket and you still cannot connect:

- ☐ – Check the clocks on the client and database server.
- ☐ – Check that the v5srvtab file exists in the correct location and is readable by Oracle. Remember to set the sqlnet.ora parameters.
- ☐ – Check that the v5srvtab file has been generated for the service named in the sqlnet.ora file on the database server side.

  ➤ If everything seems to work fine, but then you issue another query and it fails:

- ☐ – Check that the initial ticket is forwardable. You must have obtained the initial ticket by running the okinit utility.
- ☐ – Check the expiration date on the credentials. If the credentials have expired, then close the connection and run okinit to get a new initial ticket.

Conclusion

This Kerberos authentication ensures security as well as centralised authentication for the users. It is good practice to have it in the environment.

CONFIGURE SSL

SSL is an industry-standard protocol for securing network connections. You can use the Oracle Database SSL can be used to secure communications between any client and any server. For authentication, SSL uses digital certificates that comply with the X.509v3 standard and a public and private key pair. To enable SSL configuration you must configure SSL on the server, and then the client the following step explains how to configure SSL for Oracle Database.

- ➢ Introduction
- ➢ Configure SSL on the Server
- ➢ Configure SSL on the Client
- ➢ Log in to the Database Instance
- ➢ Conclusion

Introduction

SSL is an industry-standard protocol for securing network connections.SSL provides authentication, data encryption, and data integrity. The SSL protocol is the foundation of PKI. For authentication, SSL uses digital certificates that comply with the X.509v3 standard and a public and private key pair. You can use the Oracle Database SSL can be used to secure communications between any client and any server. You can configure SSL to provide authentication for the server only, the client only, or both client and server. You can also configure

SSL features in combination with other authentication methods supported by Oracle Database (database user names and passwords, RADIUS, and Kerberos).

To support your PKI implementation, Oracle Database includes the following features in addition to SSL:

- ☐ Oracle wallets, where you can store PKI credentials
- ☐ Oracle Wallet Manager, which you can use to manage your Oracle wallets
- ☐ Certificate validation with CRLs
- ☐ Hardware security module support

Configure SSL on the Server

During installation, Oracle sets defaults on the Oracle Database server and the Oracle client for SSL parameters, except the Oracle wallet location

1. Wallet Configuration on the Server
2. Specify the Database Wallet Location on the Server
3. Set SSL Client Authentication on the Server
4. Set SSL as an Authentication Service on the Server

5. Create a Listening Endpoint that Uses TCP/IP with SSL on the Server

Wallet Configuration on the Server

Before proceeding to the next step, confirm that a wallet has been created and that it has a certificate.

1. Start Oracle Wallet Manager.

2. (UNIX) From $ORACLE_HOME/bin, enter the following command:

   Owm

3. From the **Wallet** menu, select **Open**. The wallet should contain a certificate with a status of Ready and auto-login turned on. If auto-login is not on, then select it from the **Wallet** menu and save the wallet again. This turns auto-login on.

4. If wallet not created already using Oracle Wallet Manager menu, navigate to **Wallet > New**.

5. Answer **No** to: "Your default wallet directory doesn't exist. Do you wish to create it now?"

6. The new wallet screen will now prompt you to enter a password for your wallet. Be sure to make the password something you will remember. Then Click **YES** when prompted:

7. "A new empty wallet has been created. Do you wish to create a certificate request at this time?"

8. After clicking **YES** in the previous step, the "**Create Certificate Request Screen**" will appear.

   a. Enter the appropriate values.

      For example:

      Common Name: Name of your server, including the domain

      Organizational Unit: (optional) Unit within your organization

      Organization: Name of your organization

      Locality/City: Locality or city

State/Province: The full name of your State or Province (do not abbreviate)

9. Select your **Country** from the drop-down list. For the **Key Size**, select 2048 as a minimum. Click **OK**.

10. From the menu, click **Wallet** and then click **Save**.

11. On the Select Directory screen, change the directory to your fully qualified wallet directory and click **OK**.

12. From the menu, click **Wallet** and select the **Auto-Login** checkbox.

13. Exit Oracle Wallet Manager.

Specify the Database Wallet Location on the Server

Next, you are ready to specify a location on the server for the wallet.

1. Start Oracle Net Manager.

   ☐ (UNIX) From *$ORACLE_HOME*/bin, enter the following command at the command line:

   netmgr

2. Expand **Oracle Net Configuration**, and from **Local**, select **Profile**.

3. From the **Naming** list, select **Network Security**.

4. The Network Security tabbed window appears.

5. Select the **SSL** tab and then select **Configure SSL for: Server**.

6. In the **Wallet Directory** box, enter the directory in which the Oracle wallet is located or click **Browse** to find it by searching the file system. You must use that wallet to store the database PKI credentials for SSL-authenticated Enterprise User Security.

   ☐ Use Oracle Net Manager to set the wallet location in the sqlnet.ora file. Be aware that in a multitenant environment, the settings in the sqlnet.ora file applies to all pluggable databases (PDBs).

   ☐ Ensure that you enter the same wallet location when you create it and when you set the location in the sqlnet.ora file.

7. From the **File** menu, select **Save Network Configuration**.

The sqlnet.ora and listener.ora files are updated with the following entries:

wallet_location = (SOURCE=

(METHOD=File)(METHOD_DATA=(DIRECTORY=*wallet_location*)))

Set SSL Client Authentication on the Server

The SSL_CLIENT_AUTHENTICATION parameter controls whether the client is authenticated using SSL.

You must set this parameter in the sqlnet.ora file on the server. The default value of SSL_CLIENT_AUTHENTICATION parameter is TRUE. You can set the SSL_CLIENT_AUTHENTICATION to FALSE

To set SSL_CLIENT_AUTHENTICATION to TRUE on the server:

☐ In the SSL page Oracle Net Manager, select **Require Client Authentication**.
☐ From the **File** menu, select **Save Network Configuration**.

The sqlnet.ora file is updated with the following entry:

SSL_CLIENT_AUTHENTICATION=TRUE

To set SSL_CLIENT_AUTHENTICATION to FALSE on the server:

☐ In the SSL page Oracle Net Manager, select **Require Client Authentication**.
☐ From the **File** menu, select **Save Network Configuration**.

The sqlnet.ora file is updated with the following entry:

SSL_CLIENT_AUTHENTICATION=FALSE

Set SSL as an Authentication Service on the Server

The SQLNET.AUTHENTICATION_SERVICES parameter in the sqlnet.ora file sets the SSL authentication service. Set this parameter if you want to use SSL authentication in conjunction with another authentication method supported by Oracle Database. For example, use this parameter if you want the server to authenticate itself to the client by using SSL and the client to authenticate itself to the server by using Kerberos.

➢ To set the SQLNET.AUTHENTICATION_SERVICES parameter on the server, add TCP/IP with SSL (TCPS) to this parameter in the sqlnet.ora file by using a text editor.

For example, if you want to use SSL authentication in conjunction with RADIUS authentication, set this parameter as follows:

SQLNET.AUTHENTICATION_SERVICES = (TCPS, *radius*)

If you do not want to use SSL authentication in conjunction with another authentication method, then do not set this parameter.

Create a Listening Endpoint that Uses TCP/IP with SSL on the Server

You can configure a listening endpoint to use TCP/IP with SSL on the server.

➢ Configure the listener in the listener.ora file. Oracle recommends using port number 2484 for typical Oracle Net clients.

Configure SSL on the Client

When you configure SSL on the client, you configure the server DNs and use TCP/IP with SSL on the client.

1. Confirm Client Wallet Creation
2. Configure the Server DNs and Use TCP/IP with SSL on the Client
3. Specify Required Client SSL Configuration (Wallet Location)

Confirm Client Wallet Creation

You must confirm that a wallet has been created on the client and that the client has a valid certificate.

➢ Use Oracle Wallet Manager to check that the wallet has been created. See **Wallet Configuration on the Server** for information about the configuration of a wallet.

Configure the Server DNs and Use TCP/IP with SSL on the Client

You must edit the tnsnames.ora and listener.ora files to configure the server DNS and user TCP/IP with SSL on the client.

1. In the client tnsnames.ora file, add the SSL_SERVER_CERT_DN parameter and specify the database server's DN, as follows:

```
(SECURITY=

(SSL_SERVER_CERT_DN="cn=finance,cn=OracleContext,c=us,o=acme"))
```

The client uses this information to obtain the list of DNs it expects for each of the servers, enforcing the server's DN to match its service name.

The following example shows an entry for the Finance database in the tnsnames.ora file.

```
TESTSSL=

(DESCRIPTION=

(ADDRESS_LIST=

(ADDRESS= (PROTOCOL = tcps) (HOST = test_server) (PORT =1575)))

(CONNECT_DATA=

(SERVICE_NAME= Finance.us.example.com))

(SECURITY=

(SSL_SERVER_CERT_DN="cn=finance,cn=OracleContext,c=us,o=acme"))
```

By default, the tnsnames.ora and listener.ora files are in the $ORACLE_HOME/network/admin directory on UNIX systems. Alternatively, you can ensure that the common name (CN) portion of the server's DN matches the service name.

2. In the client tnsnames.ora file, enter tcps as the PROTOCOL in the ADDRESS parameter.

This specifies that the client will use TCP/IP with SSL to connect to the database that is identified in the SERVICE_NAME parameter. The following also shows an entry that specifies TCP/IP with SSL as the connecting protocol in the tnsnames.ora file.

```
LISTENER=

(DESCRIPTION_LIST=
```

```
(DESCRIPTION=

(ADDRESS=  (PROTOCOL  =  tcps)  (HOST  =  finance_server)  (PORT  =
1575))))
```

3. In the listener.ora file, enter tcps as the PROTOCOL in the ADDRESS parameter.

Specify Required Client SSL Configuration (Wallet Location)

You can use Oracle Net Manager to specify the required client SSL configuration.

1. Start Oracle Net Manager.

   ☐ (UNIX) From *$ORACLE_HOME*/bin, enter the following command at the

   ```
   command line:
   ```

   ```
   netmgr
   ```

2. Expand **Oracle** Net Configuration, and from Local, **select Profile**.
3. From the **Naming list**, select **Network Security**.

   The Network Security tabbed window appears.

4. Select the **SSL** tab.
5. Select **Configure SSL for: Client**.
6. In the Wallet Directory box, enter the directory in which the Oracle wallet is located, or click **Browse** to find it by searching the file system.
7. From the Match server X.509 name list, select one of the following options:

   ☐ **Yes:** Requires that the server's distinguished name (DN) match its service name. SSL ensures that the certificate is from the server and connections succeed only if there is a match.

   This check can be made only when RSA ciphers are selected, which is the default setting.

   ☐ **No (default):** SSL checks for a match between the DN and the service name, but does not enforce it. Connections succeed regardless of the outcome but an error is logged if the match fails.

   ☐ **Let the Client Decide:** Enables the default.

Security Alert: Not enforcing the server X.509 name match allows a server to potentially fake its identity. Oracle recommends selecting YES for this option so that connections are refused when there is a mismatch.

8. From the File menu, select Save Network Configuration.

The sqlnet.ora file on the client is updated with the following entries:

```
SSL_CLIENT_AUTHENTICATION =TRUE

wallet_location =

(SOURCE=

(METHOD=File)

(METHOD_DATA=      (DIRECTORY=wallet_location)))

SSL_SERVER_DN_MATCH=(ON/OFF)
```

Log in to the Database Instance:

After you have completed the configuration, you are ready to log in to the database.

☐ Start SQL*Plus and then enter one of the following connection commands:
   ☐ If you are using SSL authentication for the client

      (SSL_CLIENT_AUTHENTICATION=true in the sqlnet.ora file):

      CONNECT/@*net_service_name*

   ☐ If you are not using SSL authentication
      (SSL_CLIENT_AUTHENTICATION=false in the sqlnet.ora file):

      CONNECT username@net_service_name

      Enter password: password

Conclusion

The discussed configuration helps to setup the SSL for the secure network configuration. It helps in securing transaction as well as securing authentication. You can follow the above step to complete the setup of the SSL configuration.

USING ORACLE WALLET MANAGER

The **OWM** utility is a graphical user interface tool to manage wallet and certificate.

- ☐ Introduction
- ☐ Terminology and Concepts
- ☐ How SSL works with Oracle
- ☐ Wallet Password Management
- ☐ Managing Wallets
- ☐ Managing Certificates
- ☐ Conclusion

Introduction

Oracle Wallet Manager to manage public key security credentials on Oracle clients and servers. The wallets it creates can be read by Oracle Database, Oracle Application Server, and the Oracle Identity Management infrastructure.

Oracle Wallet Manager enables wallet owners to manage and edit the security credentials in their Oracle wallets. A wallet is a password-protected container used to store authentication and signing credentials, including private keys, certificates, and trusted certificates needed by SSL.

Terminology and Concepts

Transport Layer Security (TLS)

Transport Layer Security, or TLS, is the successor of SSL. TLS, like SSL, is a protocol that encrypts traffic between a client and a server. TLS creates an encrypted connection between two machines allowing for private information to be transmitted without the problems of eavesdropping, data tampering, or message forgery. There is no distinction between TLS certificates and SSL certificates issued by certifying authorities.

SSL

SSL is a technology that defines the essential functions of mutual authentication, data encryption, and data integrity for secure transactions. Exchange of data between the client

215

and server in such secure transactions is said to use the SSL. This has been deprecated in favour of TLS.

HTTP and HTTPS

HTTP is the primary communication protocol for the World Wide Web. HTTPS is a combination of HTTP and TLS.

PKI

The term PKI is used to describe the processes, technologies and practices that are required to provide a secure infrastructure. A PKI should provide the following:

- ☐ Authentication
- ☐ Non-repudiation
- ☐ Confidentiality
- ☐ Integrity
- ☐ Access Control

Certificate Authority (CA)

A CA is a trusted third party responsible for issuing, revoking, and renewing digital certificates. All digital certificates are signed with the CA's private key to ensure authenticity. The CA's Public Key is widely distributed.

Certificate Signing Request (CSR)

A CSR is a digital file which contains your public key and your name. You send the CSR to a Certifying Authority (CA) to be converted into a real certificate.

Private (Server) Key

The private key file is a digital file that you generate as part of a key pair (private key and public key) and use to encrypt/decrypt messages. The certificate request (CSR) that you send to your CA is derived from this private key. Therefore, the resulting digital certificate (containing your public key) which is issued by your CA is bound to this private key.

How SSL works with Oracle

When a network connection over Secure Sockets Layer is initiated, the client and server perform an SSL handshake before performing the authentication.

The handshake process is as follows:

1. The client and server establish which cipher suites to use. This includes which encryption algorithms are used for data transfers.
2. The server sends its certificate to the client, and the client verifies that the server's certificate was signed by a trusted CA. This step verifies the identity of the server.
3. Similarly, if client authentication is required, the client sends its own certificate to the server, and the server verifies that the client's certificate was signed by a trusted CA.
4. The client and server exchange key information using public key cryptography. Based on this information, each generates a session key. All subsequent communications between the client and the server are encrypted and decrypted by using this session key and the negotiated cipher suite.

The authentication process is as follows:

1. On a client, the user initiates an Oracle Net connection to the server by using SSL.
2. SSL performs the handshake between the client and the server.
3. If the handshake is successful, then the server verifies that the user has the appropriate authorization to access the database.

Wallet Password Management

Oracle Wallet Manager includes an enhanced wallet password management module that enforces Password Management Policy guidelines, including the following:

☐ Minimum password length (8 characters)
☐ Maximum password length unlimited
☐ Alphanumeric character mix required

Managing Wallets

This section is to describe the oracle wallet manager using different task and how it been performed , with examples

- ☐ Starting Oracle Wallet Manager
- ☐ Creating a New Wallet
- ☐ Creating a Certificate request
- ☐ Deleting the Wallet
- ☐ Changing the Password
- ☐ Using Auto-Login

Starting Oracle Wallet Manager

To start Oracle Wallet Manager:

Windows NT: Select Start—>Programs—>Oracle-<ORACLE_HOME_

NAME>—>Network Administration—>Wallet Manager

UNIX: Enter owm at the command line.

owm &

The Oracle Wallet Manager should start and display its beginning pages:

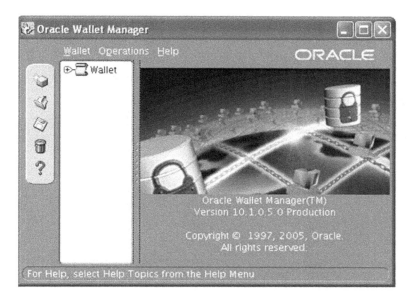

Creating a New Wallet

To create a new wallet, On the Oracle Wallet Manager menu, select Wallet and then New. Answer "No" to the question "Your default wallet directory does not exist. Do you want to create it?"

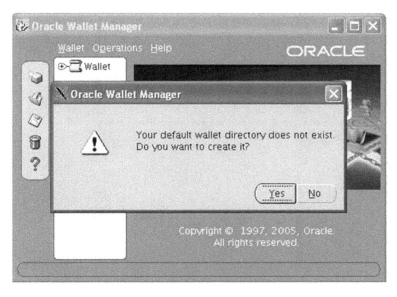

In the "New Wallet" window that appears, enter the password you would like to use for the new wallet. The orapki example used "welcome1", but any password can be used. Choose the wallet type of Standard, then click OK. This will create the initial wallet and then ask about creating a certificate request.

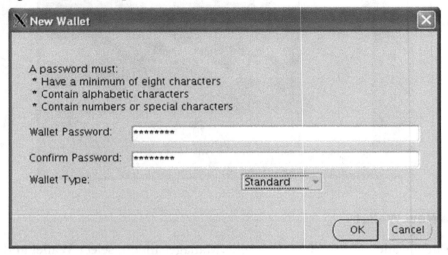

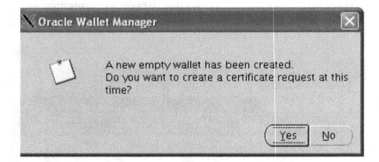

Press "YES"

Creating a Certificate request

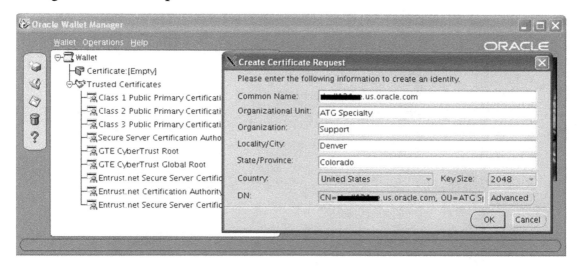

The –dn directive specifies the DN where:

CN = Common Name which can be a server (including domain) or an individual. I've hidden my actual server name in this example.

OU = Organizational Unit

O = Organization

L = Locality or City

ST = State or Province (full name, do not abbreviate)

C = Country Code

Deleting the Wallet

To delete the current open wallet:

1. Choose Wallet > Delete; the Delete Wallet dialog box appears.
2. Review the displayed wallet location to verify you are deleting the correct wallet.
3. Enter the wallet password.
4. Choose OK; a dialog panel appears to inform you that the wallet was successfully deleted.

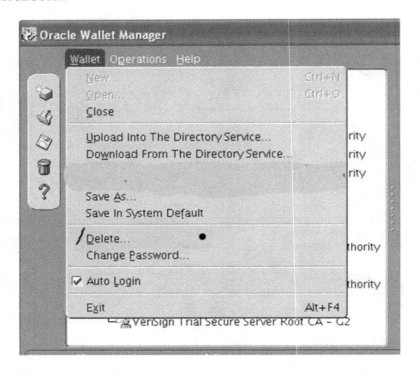

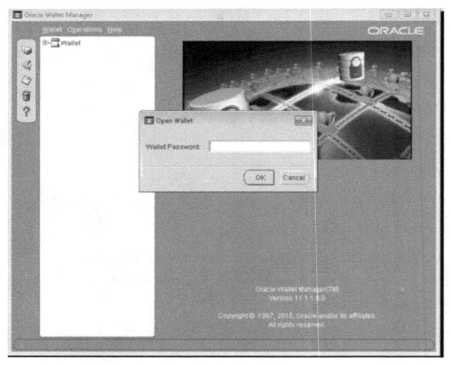

Changing the Password

A password change is effective immediately. The wallet is saved to the currently selected directory, with the new encrypted password. To change the password for the current open wallet:

1. Choose Wallet > Change Password; the Change Wallet

    A password dialog box appears.

2. Enter the existing wallet password.
3. Enter the new password.
4. Re-enter the new password.
5. Choose OK.

    A message at the bottom of the window confirms that the password was successfully changed.

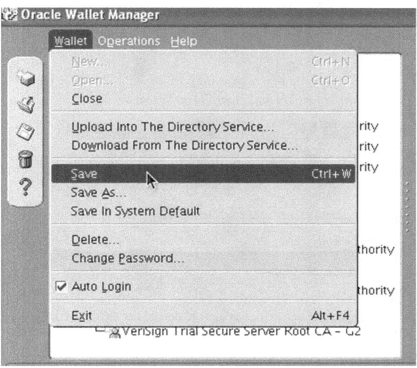

Using Auto-Login

The Oracle Wallet Manager Auto-Login feature opens a copy of the wallet and enables PKI-based access to secure services—as long as the wallet in the specified directory remains open in memory.

You must enable Auto-Login if you want single sign-on access to multiple Oracle databases (disabled by default).

To enable Auto-Login:

1. Choose Wallet from the menu bar.
2. Choose the checkbox next to the Auto-Login menu item; a message at the bottom of the window displays Auto-login enabled.

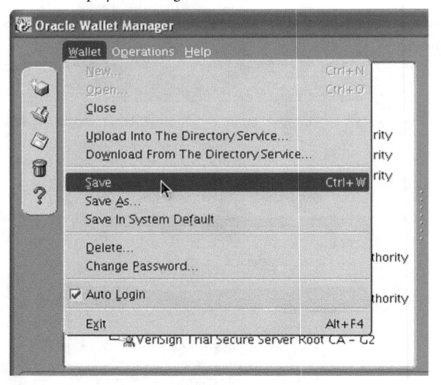

Managing Certificates

Adding a Certificate Request

Importing the User Certificate into the Wallet

Exporting a User Certificate

Exporting a User Certificate Request

Adding a Certificate Request

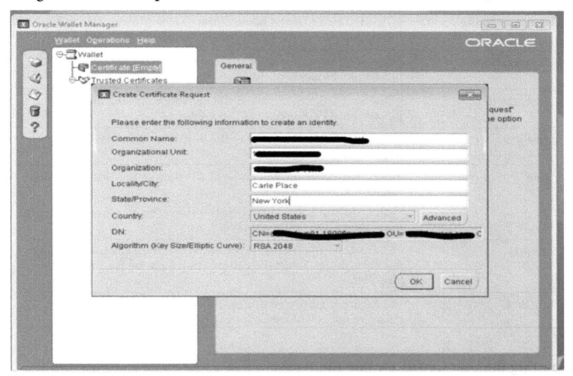

The actual certificate request becomes part of the wallet. You can reuse any certificate request to obtain a new certificate. However, you cannot edit an existing certificate request; store only a correctly filled out certificate request in a wallet.

To create a PKCS #10 certificate request:

1. Choose Operations > Add Certificate Request; the Add Certificate Request dialog box appears.

2. Choose OK. An Oracle Wallet Manager dialog box informs you that a certificate request was successfully created. You can either copy the certificate request text

from the body of this dialog panel and paste it into an email message to send to a CA, or you can export the certificate request to a file.

3. Choose OK. You are returned to the Oracle Wallet Manager main window; the status of the certificate is changed to Requested.

Field Name	Description
Common Name	Mandatory. Enter the name of the user's or service's identity. Enter a user's name in first name /last name format.
Organizational Unit	Optional. Enter the name of the identity's organizational unit. Example: Finance.
Organization	Optional.Enter the name of the identity's organization. Example: XYZ Corp.
Locality/City	Optional. Enter the name of the locality or city in which the identity resides.
State/Province	Optional. Enter the full name of the state or province in which the identity resides. Enter the full state name, because some certificate authorities do not accept two–letter abbreviations.
Country	Mandatory. Choose the drop-down list to view a list of country abbreviations. Select the country in which the organization is located.
Key Size	Mandatory. Choose the drop-down box to view a list of key sizes to use when creating the public/private key pair. See

Importing the User Certificate into the Wallet

You will receive an email notification from the CA informing you that your certificate request has been fulfilled. Import the certificate into a wallet in either of two ways: copy and paste the certificate from the email you receive from the CA, or import the user certificate from a file.

Start owm and open the wallet as before and select "Operations", "Import User Certificate". If "Import User Certificate" is greyed out, that indicates that there is no CSR as indicated by "Certificate [Requested]". If you are following these steps in order, this option should be available.

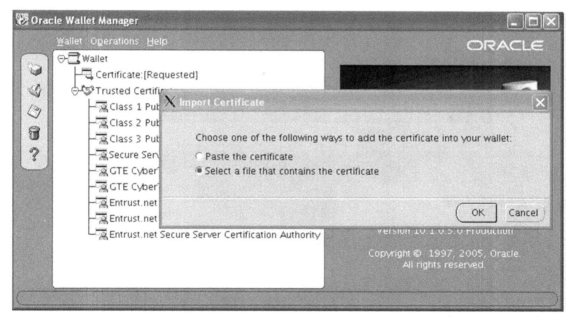

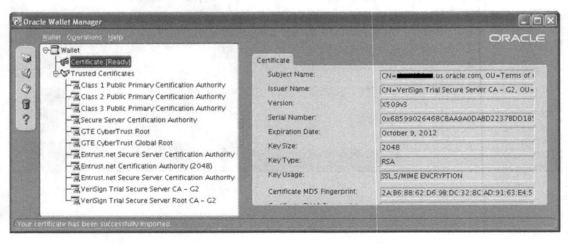

Exporting a User Certificate

Save the certificate in a file system directory when you elect to export a certificate:

1. In the left panel subtree, select the certificate that you want to export.
2. Choose Operations > Export User Certificate from the menu bar; the Export Certificate dialog box appears.
3. Enter the file system directory to save your certificate in, or navigate to the directory structure under Folders.
4. Enter a file name to save your certificate, in the Enter File Name field.
5. Choose OK. A message at the bottom of the window confirms that the certificate was successfully exported to the file. You are returned to the Oracle Wallet Manager main window.

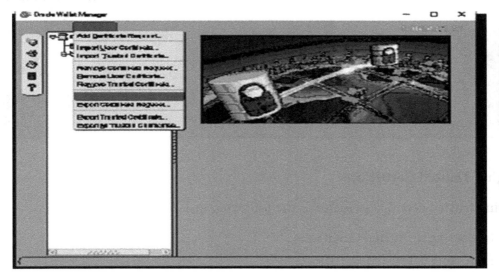

Exporting a User Certificate Request

Save the certificate request in a file system directory when you elect to export a certificate request:

1. In the left panel subtree, select the certificate request that you want to export.
2. Choose Operations > Export Certificate Request from the menu bar; the Export Certificate Request dialog box appears.

3. Enter the file system directory in which you want to save your certificate request, or navigate to the directory structure under Folders.

4. Enter a file name to save your certificate request, in the Enter File Name field.

5. Choose OK. A message at the bottom of the window confirms that the certificate request was successfully exported to the file. You are returned to the Oracle Wallet Manager main window.

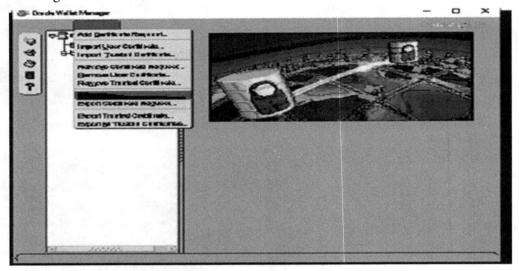

Managing Trusted Certificates

Managing trusted certificates includes the following tasks:

1. Importing a Trusted Certificate
2. Exporting a Trusted Certificate

Importing a Trusted Certificate

You can import a trusted certificate into a wallet in either of two ways: paste the trusted certificate from an email that you receive from the CA, or import the trusted certificate from a file.

Oracle Wallet Manager automatically installs trusted certificates from VeriSign, RSA, Entrust, and GTE CyberTrust when you create a new wallet.

1. Choose Operations > Import Trusted Certificate from the menu bar; the Import Trusted Certificate dialog panel appears.

2. Choose the Paste the Certificate button, and choose OK. An Import Trusted Certificate dialog panel appears with the following message: Please provide a base64 format certificate and paste it below.

3. Copy the trusted certificate from the body of the email message you received that contained the user certificate. Include the lines Begin Certificate and End Certificate.

4. Paste the certificate into the window, and Choose OK. A message at the bottom of the window informs you that the trusted certificate was successfully installed.

5. Choose OK; you are returned to the Oracle Wallet Manager main panel, and the trusted certificate appears at the bottom of the Trusted Certificates tree.

IS YOUR DATA SECURE?

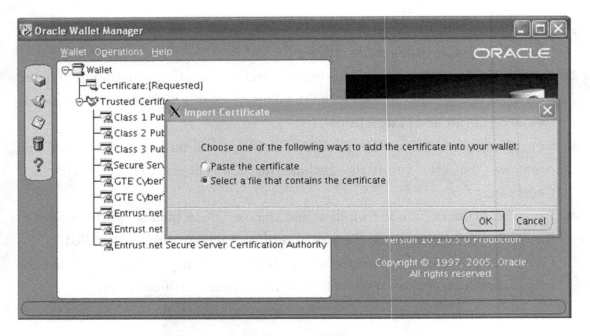

Exporting a Trusted Certificate

To export a trusted certificate to another file system location:

1. In the left panel subtree, select the trusted certificate that you want to export.
2. Select Operations > Export Trusted Certificate; the Export Trusted Certificate dialog box appears.
3. Enter a file system directory in which you want to save your trusted certificate, or navigate to the directory structure under Folders.
4. Enter a file name to save your trusted certificate.
5. Choose OK; you are returned to the Oracle Wallet Manager main window.

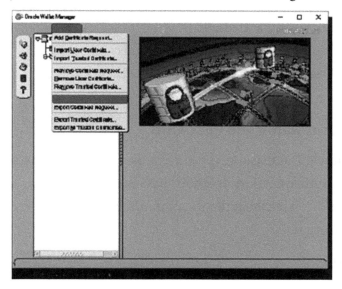

Conclusion

In this chapter, you have learned how to manage wallet and certificate using an oracle wallet manager.

CONFIGURING MULTIPLE AUTHENTICATION METHODS AND DISABLING ORACLE STRONG AUTHENTICATION

Introduction

This chapter describes how to configure multiple authentication methods under Oracle Network Security, and how to use the conventional user name and password authentication, even if you have configured another authentication method. This also chapter describes how to configure your network so that Oracle clients can use a specific authentication method and Oracle servers can accept any method specified.

- ☐ Connecting with User Name and Password
- ☐ Disabling Security Authentication
- ☐ Configuring Multiple Authentication Methods
- ☐ Configuring Oracle Database for External Authentication
- ☐ Conclusion

Connecting with User Name and Password

To connect to an Oracle Database server using a user name and password when an Oracle Advanced Security authentication method has been configured, disable the external authentication, With the external authentication disabled, a user can connect to a database using the following format:

$ sqlplus hr@emp

Enter password: password

Note: You can configure multiple authentication methods, including both externally authenticated users and password-authenticated users, on a single database.

Disabling Security Authentication

Use Oracle Net Manager to disable authentication methods. Navigate to profile and select Network security.

- ☐ Click the Authentication tab

- ☐ Sequentially move all authentication methods from the Selected Method list to the Available Methods list by selecting a method and choosing the left arrow [<]
- ☐ Select File, then Save Network Configuration
- ☐ The sqlnet.ora file is updated with the following entry:

SQLNET.AUTHENTICATION_SERVICES = (NONE)

Network Security tabbed window is displayed in the below image.

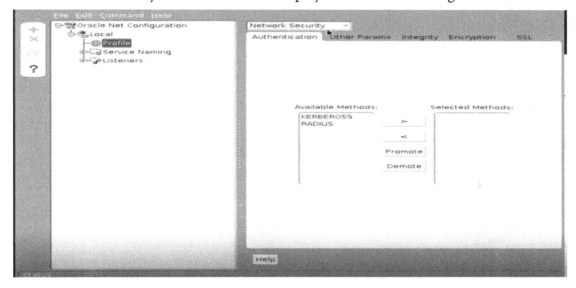

Configuring Multiple Authentication Methods

Many networks use more than one authentication method on a single security server. Accordingly, Oracle Advanced Security lets you configure your network so that Oracle clients can use a specific authentication method, and Oracle Database servers can accept any method specified. You can set up multiple authentication methods on both client and server systems either by using Oracle Net Manager, or by using any text editor to modify the sqlnet.ora file.

Use Oracle Net Manager to add authentication methods to both clients and servers

Following steps describe how to configure Multiple authentication Methods.

- ☐ Navigate to the profile.

- [ ] Click the Authentication tab.
- [ ] Sequentially move all authentication methods from the Selected Method list to the Available Methods list by selecting a method and choosing the left arrow [>].
- [ ] Arrange the selected methods in order of desired use. To do this, select a method in the Selected Methods list, and select Promote or Demote to position it in the list.
- [ ] Select File, then Save Network Configuration.
- [ ] The sqlnet.ora file is updated with the following entry, listing the selected authentication methods:

SQLNET.AUTHENTICATION_SERVICES = (KERBEROS5, RADIUS)

Note: SecurID functionality is available through RADIUS; RADIUS support is built into the RSA ACE/Server.

Configuring Oracle Database for External Authentication

This section describes the parameters you must set to configure Oracle Database for network authentication, using the following tasks:

Setting the SQLNET.AUTHENTICATION_SERVICES Parameter in sqlnet.ora

Setting OS_AUTHENT_PREFIX to a Null Value

Setting the SQLNET.AUTHENTICATION_SERVICES Parameter in sqlnet.ora

The following parameter must be set in the sqlnet.ora file for all clients and servers to enable each to use a supported authentication method:

SQLNET.AUTHENTICATION_SERVICES=(oracle_authentication_method)

For example, for all clients and servers using Kerberos authentication, the sqlnet.ora parameter must be set as follows:

SQLNET.AUTHENTICATION_SERVICES=(KERBEROS5)

Setting OS_AUTHENT_PREFIX to a Null Value

Authentication service-based user names can be long, and Oracle user names are limited to 30 characters. Oracle strongly recommends that you enter a null value for the

OS_AUTHENT_PREFIX parameter in the initialization file used for the database instance as follows:

OS_AUTHENT_PREFIX="""

Note: The default value for OS_AUTHENT_PREFIX is OPS$; however, you can set it to any string

Attention: If a database already has the OS_AUTHENT_PREFIX set to a value other than NULL (" "), do not change it, because it can inhibit previously created, externally identified users from connecting to the Oracle server.

To create a user, launch SQL*Plus and enter the following

SQL> CREATE USER os_authent_prefix username IDENTIFIED EXTERNALLY;

When OS_AUTHENT_PREFIX is set to a null value (" "), enter the following to create the user ram:

SQL> CREATE USER ram IDENTIFIED EXTERNALLY;

The advantage of creating a user in this way is that the administrator no longer needs to maintain different user names for externally identified users. This is true for all supported authentication methods.

Conclusion

With this discussion you can easily understand ,How to configuring the secure user and disabling the strong authentication and creating multiple authentications and so on.

INTEGRATING AUTHENTICATION DEVICES USING RADIUS

The RADIUS challenge-response user interface further enhances authentication in a RADIUS configuration.

- ☐ Introduction
- ☐ Customizing the RADIUS Challenge-Response User Interface
- ☐ Example: Using the OracleRadiusInterface Interface
- ☐ Conclusion

Introduction

You can set up any authentication device that supports the RADIUS standard to authenticate Oracle users. You can also use third-party authentication vendors to customise the RADIUS challenge-response user interface to fit for a device. When your authentication device uses the challenge-response mode, a graphical interface prompts the end-user first for a password and then for additional information. This interface is Java-based to provide optimal platform independence. Third-party vendors of authentication devices must customise this graphical user interface to fit their device. For example, a smart card vendor customises the Oracle client to issue the challenge to the smart card reader. Then, when the smart card receives a challenge, it responds by prompting the user for more information such as a PIN.

Customizing the RADIUS Challenge-Response User Interface

You can customise OracleRadiusInterface interface by creating your own class.

1. Open the sqlnet.ora file.

   By default, the sqlnet.ora file is located in the *ORACLE_HOME*/network/admin directory or in the location set by the TNS_ADMIN environment variable. Ensure that you have properly set the TNS_ADMIN variable to point to the correct sqlnet.ora file.

2. Locate the SQLNET.RADIUS_AUTHENTICATION_INTERFACE parameter, and replace the name of the class listed there (DefaultRadiusInterface), with the name of the new class that you have created. When you make this change in the sqlnet.ora file, the class is loaded on the Oracle client in order to handle the authentication process.

3. Save and exit the sqlnet.ora file

   The third-party must implement the OracleRadiusInterface interface, which is located in the ORACLE.NET.RADIUS package.

Example: Using the OracleRadiusInterface Interface

You can use the OracleRadiusInterface interface to retrieve a user name and password.

Using the OracleRadiusInterface Interface

public interface OracleRadiusInterface {

public void radiusRequest();

public void radiusChallenge(String challenge);

public String getUserName();

public String getPassword();

}

In this specification:

- ➤ radiusRequest prompts the end-user for a user name and password, which will later be retrieved through getUserName and getPassword.
- ➤ getUserName extracts the user name the user enters. If this method returns an empty string, it is assumed that the user wants to cancel the operation. The user then receives a message indicating that the authentication attempt failed.
- ➤ getPassword extracts the password the user enters. If getUserName returns a valid string, but getPassword returns an empty string, the challenge keyword is replaced as the password by the database. If the user enters a valid password, a challenge may or may not be returned by the RADIUS server.
- ➤ radiusChallenge presents a request sent from the RADIUS server for the user to respond to the server's challenge.
- ➤ getResponse extracts the response the user enters. If this method returns a valid response, then that information populates the User-Password attribute in the new Access-Request packet. If an empty string is returned, the operation is aborted from both sides by returning the corresponding value.

Conclusion

In this chapter you have learned how to customise the device to support the RADIUS authentication and how to use RADIUS Interface.

ORACLE DATABASE FIPS 140-2 SETTINGS

Oracle supports the FIPS standard for 140-2.

- ☐ Introduction
- ☐ Configuring FIPS For TDE and DBMS_CRYPTO
- ☐ Configuration of FIPS for SSL
- ☐ Post-installation Checklist for FIPS 140-2
- ☐ Verifying FIPS 140-2 Connections
- ☐ Conclusion

Introduction

The FIPS standard, 140-2, is a U.S. government standard that defines cryptographic module security requirements.

The FIPS 140-2 cryptographic libraries are designed to protect data at rest and in transit over the network.Oracle Database uses these cryptographic libraries for SSL,TDE, and DBMS_CRYPTO PL/SQL package.To verify the current status of the certification, you can find information at the Computer Security Resource Centre (CSRC) Web site address from the National Institute of Standards and Technology:

http://csrc.nist.gov/groups/STM/cmvp/validation.html

You can find information specific to FIPS by searching for Validated FIPS 140 Cryptographic Modules. The security policy, which is available on this site upon successful certification, includes requirements for secure configuration of the host operating system.

Configuring FIPS for TDE and DBMS_CRYPTO

The DBFIPS_140 initialization parameter configures FIPS mode.

1. To configure TDE and the DBMS_CRYPTO PL/SQL package program units to run in FIPS mode, set the DBFIPS_140 initialization parameter to TRUE.

   The effect of this parameter depends on the platform.

2. Restart the database.

Platform	Effect of Setting DBFIPS_140 to TRUE or FALSE
Linux or Windows on Intel x86_64	* TRUE: TDE and DBMS_CRYPTO program units use Micro Edition Suite (MES) 4.0.5.1 FIPS mode
	* FALSE: TDE and DBMS_CRYPTO program units use Intel Performance Primitives (IPP)

Be aware that setting DBFIPS_140 to TRUE and thus using the underlying library in FIPS mode incurs a certain amount of overhead when the library is first loaded. This is due to the verification of the signature and the execution of the self-tests on the library. Once the library is loaded, then there is no other impact on performance.

Configuration of FIPS for SSL

The SSLFIPS_140 parameter configures the SSL.

- ☐ Configuring the SSLFIPS_140 Parameter for Secure Sockets Layer
- ☐ Approved SSL Cipher Suites for FIPS 140-2

Configuring the SSLFIPS_140 Parameter for Secure Sockets Layer

Setting the SSLFIPS_140 parameter to TRUE in the fips.ora file configures the SSL adapter to run in FIPS mode.

1. Ensure that the fips.ora file is either located in the *$ORACLE_HOME*/ldap/admin directory, or is in a location pointed to by the FIPS_HOME environment variable.
2. In the fips.ora file, set SSLFIPS_140. For example, to set SSLFIPS_140 to TRUE: SSLFIPS_140=TRUE
3. This parameter is set to FALSE by default. You must set it to TRUE on both the client and the server for FIPS mode operation.
4. Repeat this procedure in any Oracle Database home for any database server or client. When you set SSLFIPS_140 to TRUE, Secure Sockets Layer cryptographic operations take place in the embedded RSA/MES library in FIPS mode.

5. These cryptographic operations are accelerated by the CPU when hardware acceleration is available and properly configured in the host hardware and software. If you set SSLFIPS_140 to FALSE, then Secure Sockets Layer cryptographic operations take place in the embedded RSA/MES library in *non*-FIPS mode, and as with the TRUE setting, the operations are accelerated.

6. if possible. For native encryption, this behaviour of cryptographic operations landing in RSA/MES and being accelerated is similar to the above, except that it is determined by the FIPS_140 setting in sqlnet.ora (instead of the SSL_FIPS140 setting in fips.ora).

Note: The SSLFIPS_140 parameter replaces the SQLNET.SSLFIPS_140 parameter used in Oracle Database 10*g* release 2 (10.2). You must set the parameter in the fips.ora file, and not the sqlnet.ora file.

Approved SSL Cipher Suites for FIPS 140-2

A cipher suite is a set of authentication, encryption, and data integrity algorithms that exchange messages between network nodes. During an SSL handshake, for example, the two nodes negotiate to see as to which cipher suite they will use when transmitting messages back and forth.

Only the following cipher suites are approved for FIPS validation:

➢ SSL_DH_anon_WITH_3DES_EDE_CBC_SHA
➢ SSL_RSA_WITH_AES_256_CBC_SHA
➢ SSL_RSA_WITH_AES_128_CBC_SHA
➢ SSL_RSA_WITH_AES_256_GCM_SHA384
➢ SSL_RSA_WITH_3DES_EDE_CBC_SHA

Oracle Database SSL cipher suites are automatically set to FIPS approved cipher suites. If you wish to configure specific cipher suites, you can do so by editing the SSL_CIPHER_SUITES parameter in the sqlnet.ora or the listener.ora file.

SSL_CIPHER_SUITES=(SSL_cipher_suite1[,SSL_cipher_suite2[,…]])

You can also use Oracle Net Manager to set this parameter on the server and the client.

Post-installation Checklist for FIPS 140-2

After you configure the FIPS 140-2 settings, you must verify permissions in the operating system.

The permissions are as follows:

➢ Set execute permissions on all Oracle executable files to prevent the execution of Oracle Cryptographic Libraries by users who are unauthorised to do so, in accordance with the system security policy.

➢ Set the read and write permissions on all Oracle executable files to prevent accidental or deliberate reading or modification of Oracle Cryptographic Libraries by any user.

To comply with FIPS 140-2 Level 2 requirements, in the security policy, including procedures to prevent unauthorised users from reading, modifying or executing Oracle Cryptographic Libraries processes and the memory they are using in the operating system.

Verifying FIPS 140-2 Connections

To check if FIPS mode is enabled for SSL, you can enable tracing in the sqlnet.ora file.

You can find FIPS self-test messages in the trace file.

1. Add the following lines to sqlnet.ora to enable tracing:

    trace_directory_server=*trace_directory*

    trace_file_server=*trace_file*

    trace_level_server=*trace_level*

    For example:

    trace_directory=/private/oracle/owm

    trace_file_server=fips_trace.trc

    trace_level_server=6

2. To check if FIPS mode is enabled for TDE and DBMS_CRYPTO, log into SQL*Plus and run the following command:

SHOW PARAMETER DBFIPS_140

Trace level 6 is the minimum trace level required to check the results of the FIPS selftests.

Conclusion

It is a good option to consider enabling in the implementation of TDE, SSL because recent day data is theft over the network very easily. So when we setup this standard automatically the cryptographic operations take place in the embedded RSA/MES,So message going over the network well protected.

ORAPKI UTILITY

The orapki utility, a command-line tool to manage CRLs, create and manage Oracle wallets, and create signed certificates for testing purposes

- ☐ Introduction
- ☐ Creating Signed Certificates for Testing Purposes
- ☐ Managing Oracle Wallets with orapki Utility
- ☐ Managing CRLs with orapki Utility
- ☐ Conclusion

Introduction

The orapki utility is provided to manage PKI elements, such as wallets and CRLs, on the command line so the tasks it performs can be incorporated into scripts. This enables you to automate many of the routine tasks of maintaining a PKI.

This command-line utility can be used to perform the following tasks:

1. Creating signed certificates for testing purposes
2. Managing Oracle wallets:
   - ☐ Creating and displaying Oracle wallets
   - ☐ Adding and removing certificate requests
   - ☐ Adding and removing certificates

    ☐ Adding and removing trusted certificates

3. Managing CRLs:

    ☐ Renaming CRLs with a hash value for certificate validation

    ☐ Uploading, listing, viewing, and deleting CRLs in Oracle Internet Directory

orapki allows you to import certificates in both DER and PEM formats.

Creating Signed Certificates for Testing Purposes

This command-line utility provides a convenient, lightweight way to create signed certificates for testing purposes. The following syntax can be used to create signed certificates and to view certificates:

To create a signed certificate for testing purposes:

orapki cert create [-wallet wallet_location] -request

certificate_request_location

-cert certificate_location -validity number_of_days [-summary]

This command creates a signed certificate from the certificate request. The -wallet parameter specifies the wallet containing the user certificate and private key that will be used to sign the certificate request. The -validity parameter specifies the number of days, starting from the current date, that this certificate will be valid. Specifying a certificate and certificate request is mandatory for this command.

Ex: Wallet creation with auto_login

orapki wallet create -wallet /u01/app/oracle/12102/wallet -pwd paske123 -auto_login

Oracle PKI Tool : Version 12.1.0.2

Copyright (c) 2004, 2014, Oracle and/or its affiliates. All rights reserved.

To view a certificate:

orapki cert display -cert certificate_location [-summary | -complete]

This command enables you to view a test certificate that you have created with orapki. You can choose either -summary or -complete, which determines how much detail the command will display. If you choose -summary, the command will display the certificate and its expiration date. If you choose -complete, it will display additional certificate information, including the serial number and public key.

> Ex:
>
> orapki wallet display -wallet "/u01/app/oracle/12102/wallet" -pwd paske123
>
> Oracle PKI Tool : Version 12.1.0.2
>
> Copyright (c) 2004, 2014, Oracle and/or its affiliates. All rights reserved.
>
> Requested Certificates:
>
> User Certificates:
>
> Trusted Certificates:
>
> Subject: CN=DigiCert SHA2 Secure Server CA,O=DigiCert Inc,C=US
>
> Subject: CN=DigiCert Global Root CA,OU=www.digicert.com,O=DigiCert Inc,C=US

Managing Oracle Wallets with the orapki Utility

The following sections describe the syntax used to create and manage Oracle wallets with the orapki command-line utility. You can use these orapki utility wallet module commands in scripts to automate the wallet creation process.

> Creating and Viewing Oracle Wallets with orapki
>
> Adding Certificates and Certificate Requests to Oracle Wallets with orapki
>
> Exporting Certificates and Certificate Requests from Oracle Wallets with orapki
>
> Creating and Viewing Oracle Wallets with orapki

To create an Oracle wallet

> orapki wallet create -wallet wallet_location

This command will prompt you to enter and re-enter a wallet password. It creates a wallet in the location specified for -wallet.

To create an Oracle wallet with auto-login enabled

orapki wallet create -wallet wallet_location -auto_login

This command creates a wallet with auto-login enabled, or it can also be used to enable auto-login on an existing wallet. If the wallet_location already contains a wallet, then auto-login will be enabled for it. To disable the auto-login feature, delete cwallet.sso.

To view an Oracle wallet

orapki wallet display -wallet wallet_location

This command displays the certificate requests, user certificates, and trusted certificates contained in the wallet.

Adding Certificates and Certificate Requests to Oracle Wallets with orapki

To add a certificate request to an Oracle wallet

orapki wallet add -wallet wallet_location -dn user_dn -keysize 512|1024|2048|4096

This command adds a certificate request to a wallet for the user with the specified DN (user_dn). The request also specifies the requested certificate's key size (512, 1024, or 2048 bits).

To add a trusted certificate to an Oracle wallet

orapki wallet add -wallet wallet_location -trusted_cert -cert certificate_location

This command adds a trusted certificate, at the specified location (-cert *certificate_location*), to a wallet. You must add all trusted certificates in the certificate chain of a user certificate before adding a user certificate, or the command to add the user certificate will fail.

Ex: Adding Trusted certificate:

orapki wallet add -wallet /u01/app/oracle/12102/wallet -trusted_cert -cert "/export/home/oracle/JK/13_SEP_19/SubDigiCert.cer" -pwd pkers123

Oracle PKI Tool : Version 12.1.0.2

To add a root certificate to an Oracle wallet

orapki wallet add -wallet wallet_location -dn certificate_dn -keysize 512|1024|2048 -self_signed -validity number_of_days

This command creates a new self-signed (root) certificate and adds it to the wallet. The -validity parameter (mandatory) specifies the number of days, starting from the current date, that this certificate will be valid. You can specify a key size for this root certificate (-keysize) of 512, 1024, 2048, or 4096 bits.

To add a user certificate to an Oracle wallet:

orapki wallet add -wallet wallet_location -user_cert -cert certificate_location

This command adds the user certificate at the location specified with the -cert parameter to the Oracle wallet at the *wallet_location*. Before you add a user certificate to a wallet, you must add all of the trusted certificates that make up the certificate chain. If all trusted certificates are not installed in the wallet before you add the user certificate, then adding the user certificate will fail.

Exporting Certificates and Certificate Requests from Oracle Wallets with orapki

To export a certificate from an Oracle wallet

orapki wallet export -wallet wallet_location -dn certificate_dn -cert certificate_filename

This command exports a certificate with the subject's DN (-dn) from a wallet to a file that is specified by -cert.

To export a certificate request from an Oracle wallet

orapki wallet export -wallet wallet_location -dn certificate_request_dn -request certificate_request_filename

This command exports a certificate request with the subject's DN (-dn) from a wallet to a file that is specified by -request.

Managing CRLs with orapki Utility

CRLs must be managed with orapki. This utility creates a hashed value of the CRL issuer's name to identify the CRLs location in your system. If you do not use orapki, your Oracle server cannot locate CRLs to validate PKI digital certificates. The following sections describe CRLs, how you use them, and how to use orapki to manage them:

1. "About Certificate Validation with CRLs"
2. "CRLs Management"

About Certificate Validation with CRLs

The process of determining whether a given certificate can be used in a given context is referred to as certificate validation. Certificate validation includes determining that:

A trusted CA has digitally signed the certificate.

The certificate's digital signature corresponds to the independently-calculated hash value of the certificate itself and the certificate signer's (CA's) public key.

The certificate has not expired.

The certificate has not been revoked.

The SSL network layer automatically performs the first three validation checks, but you must configure the CRL checking to ensure that certificates have not been revoked. CRLs are signed data structures that contain a list of revoked certificates. They are usually issued and signed by the same entity who issued the original certificate.

CRLs Management

Before you can enable certificate revocation status checking, you must ensure that the CRLs you receive from the CAs you use are in a form (renamed with a hash value) or in a location (uploaded to the directory) in which your system can use them. Oracle Advanced Security provides a command-line utility, orapki, that you can use to perform the following tasks:

☐ Renaming CRLs with a Hash Value for Certificate Validation
☐ Uploading CRLs to Oracle Internet Directory

   ☐ Listing CRLs Stored in Oracle Internet Directory

   ☐ Viewing CRLs in Oracle Internet Directory

   ☐ Deleting CRLs from Oracle Internet Directory

Renaming CRLs with a Hash Value for Certificate Validation

When the system validates a certificate, it must locate the CRL issued by the CA who created the certificate. The system locates the appropriate CRL by matching the issuer name in the certificate with the issuer name in the CRL.

When you specify a CRL storage location for the Certificate Revocation Lists Path field in Oracle Net Manager (sets the **SSL_CRL_PATH** parameter in the sqlnet.ora file), use the orapki utility to rename CRLs with a hash value that represents the issuer's name. Creating the hash value enables the server to load the CRLs.

On UNIX systems, orapki creates a symbolic link to the CRL. On Windows systems, it creates a copy of the CRL file. In either case, the symbolic link or the copy created by orapki are named with a hash value of the issuer's name. Then when the system validates a certificate, the same hash function is used to calculate the link (or copy) name so the appropriate CRL can be loaded.

Depending on your operating system, enter one of the following commands to rename CRLs stored in the file system.

To rename CRLs stored in UNIX file systems:

      orapki crl hash -crl crl_filename [-wallet wallet_location]

      -symlink crl_directory [-summary]

In the preceding commands, crl_filename is the name of the CRL file, *wallet_location* is the location of a wallet that contains the certificate of the CA that issued the CRL, and *crl_directory* is the directory in which the CRL is located.

Using -wallet and -summary is optional. Specifying -wallet causes the tool to verify the validity of the CRL against the CA's certificate prior to renaming the CRL. Specifying the -summary option causes the tool to display the CRL issuer's name.

Uploading CRLs to Oracle Internet Directory

Publishing CRLs in the directory enables CRL validation throughout your enterprise, eliminating the need for individual applications to configure their own CRLs. All applications can use the CRLs stored in the directory in which they can be centrally managed, greatly reducing the administrative overhead of CRL management and use.

The user who uploads CRLs to the directory by using orapki must be a member of the directory group CRLAdmins (cn=CRLAdmins,cn=groups,%s_OracleContextDN%). This is a privileged operation because these CRLs are accessible to the entire enterprise. Contact your directory administrator to be added to this administrative directory group.

To upload CRLs to the directory, enter the following at the command line:

orapki crl upload -crl crl_location

-ldap hostname:ssl_port -user username [-wallet wallet_location] [-summary]

In the preceding command, *crl_location* is the file name or URL in which the CRL is located, *hostname* and *ssl_port* (SSL port with no authentication) are for the system on which your directory is installed, *username* is the directory user who has permission to add CRLs to the CRL subtree, and *wallet_location* is the location of a wallet that contains the certificate of the CA that issued the CRL.

Using -wallet and -summary is optional. Specifying -wallet causes the tool to verify the validity of the CRL against the CA's certificate prior to uploading it to the directory. Specifying the -summary option causes the tool to print the CRL issuer's name and the LDAP entry in which the CRL is stored in the directory.

Listing CRLs Stored in Oracle Internet Directory

You can display a list of all CRLs stored in the directory with orapki, which is useful for browsing to locate a particular CRL to view or download to your local system. This command displays the CA who issued the CRL (Issuer) and its location (DN) in the CRL subtree of your directory.

To list CRLs in Oracle Internet Directory, enter the following at the command line:

IS YOUR DATA SECURE?

orapki crl list -ldap hostname:ssl_port

In the preceding command, the *hostname* and *ssl_port* are for the system on which your directory is installed.

To view a summary listing of a CRL in Oracle Internet Directory, enter the following at the command line:

orapki crl display -crl crl_location [-wallet wallet_location] -summary

In the preceding command, *crl_location* is the location of the CRL in the directory. It is convenient to paste the CRL location from the list that displays when you use the orapki crl list command.

To view a list of all revoked certificates contained in a specified CRL, which is stored in Oracle Internet Directory, enter the following at the command line:

orapki crl display -crl crl_location [-wallet wallet_location] -complete

Using the -wallet option causes the orapki crl display command to validate the CRL against the CA's certificate.Depending on the size of your CRL, choosing the -complete option may take a long time to display.

To delete CRLs from the directory, enter the following at the command line:

orapki crl delete -issuer issuer_name -ldap hostname:ssl_port -user username [-summary]

In the preceding command, *issuer_name* is the name of the CA who issued the CRL, the *hostname* and *ssl_port* are for the system on which your directory is installed, and *username* is the directory user who has permission to delete CRLs from the CRL subtree. Note that this must be a directory SSL port with no authentication

Conclusion

In this chapter you have learned how to use the orapki utility for managing the trusted certificate and How to manage CRLs.

252

REFERENCE

1. https://docs.oracle.com/cd/B28359_01/network.111/b28531/guidelines.htm#DBSEG009

2. https://docs.oracle.com/cd/B28359_01/network.111/b28531/authentication.htm# DBSEG003

3. https://docs.oracle.com/en/database/oracle/oracle-database/12.2/dbseg/database-security-guide.pdf

4. https://docs.oracle.com/cd/B28359_01/network.111/b28531/guidelines.htm#DBSEG009

5. https://docs.oracle.com/cd/B28359_01/network.111/b28531/authentication.htm# DBSEG003

i. Data reference
https://docs.oracle.com/cd/B28359_01/network.111/b28531/vpd.htm#DBSEG98237

ii. Data reference

https://www.giac.org/paper/gsec/2692/oracles-virtual-private-database/102024

iii. Code reference https://oracle-base.com/articles/8i/virtual-private-databases

6. https://docs.oracle.com/en/database/oracle/oracle-database/12.2/dbseg/database-security-uide.pdf

SSL Primer: Enabling SSL in Oracle E-Business Suite Release 12 (Trial Certificate Example) (Doc ID 1425103.1)

Enabling TLS in Oracle E-Business Suite Release 12.2 (Doc ID 1367293.1).

7. https://docs.oracle.com/database/121/DBIMI/wallet.htm#DBIMI160

https://docs.oracle.com/en/database/oracle/oracle-database/12.2/dbseg/database-security-guide.pdf

https://docs.oracle.com/en/database/oracle/oracle-database/12.2/dbseg/database-security-guide.pdf

https://docs.oracle.com/en/database/oracle/oracle-database/12.2/dbseg/database-security-guide.pdf

https://docs.oracle.com/en/database/oracle/oracle-database/12.2/dbseg/database-security-guide.pdf

AUDITING AND LOGGING

OVERVIEW AUDITING AND LOGGING

One of the most threatening challenges for today's businesses are

☐ Risk of security breaches

☐ Satisfying compliance regulations

Unauthorised access, use, or disclosure of sensitive and critical information can seriously impact the business

Important regulations, such as the Sarbanes-Oxley Act (SOX) , Health Insurance Portability and Accountability Act (HIPAA), Payment Card Industry Data Security Standard (PCI-DSS) etc have resulted in information protection and becoming a top-level issue for the enterprise.

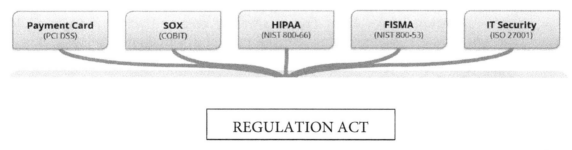

| Payment Card (PCI DSS) | SOX (COBIT) | HIPAA (NIST 800-66) | FISMA (NIST 800-53) | IT Security (ISO 27001) |

REGULATION ACT

As security threats become more sophisticated and complicated , monitoring is becoming an increasingly important component in each and every aspect in business

There should be some framework specifically designed to help clients meet compliance and security standards such as SOX, Payment Card Industry (PCI), FISMA, and HIPAA

Oracle E-Business Suite and its associated technology stack provide a variety of frameworks such as auditing and logging features to address different security threats. This document is intended to introduce and describe the various auditing and logging mechanisms available, what tasks they should be leveraged for, and recommendations for how to configure them in the context of Oracle E-Business Suite. These features are sophisticated and are able to satisfy almost all an organization's compliance and security requirements.

To make it easy for clients to implement this auditing and logging features, EBS framework has a lot of maturity levels – which level a client starts at depends on the infrastructure and policies they follow.

The auditing and logging features will be used to analyse the following:

- Historical Events
- Recent and current Events
- Unexpected Events

Historical Events

Retain historical data about what has been changed with respect to EBS

Oracle EBS Audit Trail - Audit Trail is a way of keeping track of changes made to important data in Oracle EBS application tables. It keeps a history of the following things:

- What changed
- Who changed
- When the change happened
- Database Auditing - Monitors and records configured database actions. It can be used to track table changes, in a manner similar to the Audit Trail feature discussed above.
- Fine-Grained Auditing - Allows detailed conditions to trigger auditing of data access based on content.

☐ Proxy User Auditing - This default auditing feature gives the usage of the Oracle E-Business Suite Proxy User with reports that can be used to audit the use of this feature.

☐ Page Access Tracking - Gives you historical information like what users were doing and what the performance was. It also gives us what a specific user and sessions were accessing.

☐ OHS Apache Access Logs - This default auditing feature keeps tracks all HTTP GET requests that come into Oracle EBS with their parameters.

☐ Database Listener Logs - This keeps track all database listener commands and connections to the database.

Recent and Current Events

"Recent and Current Activity" explains what is happening in the system currently, or what the last activity was performed.

☐ Records information about who and when each record was created and last updated

☐ Records information about each user session, as well as the last activity performed on that session

☐ Records Oracle E-Business Suite session information in v$session

Unexpected Events

"Unexpected events" are events or reports which we get in certain areas of oracle EBS like unsuccessful login attempts, unexpected connection or Database errors etc

☐ Unsuccessful Login Attempts - Captures detailed information about unsuccessful login attempts

☐ Debug Logging (Unexpected Logging) - Captures debug information at a variety of levels

☐ OHS Apache Error Logs - Captures unexpected events that occur at the Oracle HTTP Server level

☐ Oracle Database Listener Log - Captures unexpected connection errors

☐ Oracle Database Alert Log - Captures unexpected database errors

Conclusion

One of the most valuable assets in an organization is data and it is stored in their enterprise applications is critical to every aspect of the day-to-day running of the business. Accountability is essential in corporate governance and regulation. All organizations need the ability to be able to account for the state of all of their sensitive and critical data at any time. Oracle E-Business Suite and its associated technology stack provide auditing and logging features to address different aspects to fulfil the above said accountability.

WHAT AND WHY AUDITING AND LOGGING

Auditing

Simply put, an audit is a chronological record of change. Auditing is about tracking the use of database records and authority. When you audit each operation on the data can be monitored and logged to an audit trail, including information about which database object or data record was touched, what account performed the action and when the activity occurred.

Creating an audit trail is just a case of ensuring that whenever something is changed, a record of the change is stored; then later, you can look back in time and see a full history of what was changed, by whom and when. During an audit, the auditor (internal or external) may ask for evidence that you are correctly following your change management processes, or they may ask for evidence that you know who has changed something and when.

Without an audit trail in place, you are not able to provide this kind of information.

Logging

A "log" is a collection of messages which is used to get a picture of an event or occurrence which had occurred

Why Audit and Logging?

For organizations, the data stored in their ERP is very critical in day-to-day running of the business and the data may be relating to SCM,FINANCIALS,HRMS,MANUFACTURING etc and the list goes on and on.

Accountability in corporate governance and regulation with the ability to be able to account for the state of all of their sensitive and critical data at any time is crucial and mandatory. To provide this sort of accountability of change Oracle EBS provides the feature called "AUDITING AND LOGGING".

There are many different reasons for configuring an Oracle E-Business Suite environment for auditing and logging. It is generally recognised that a well-managed audit and logging is a key indicator of a good internal control environment. Your ability to answer very detailed questions about what's going on in your oracle EBS can make or break a compliance audit or security investigation. Aside from the obvious need for this information in the event of a breach, it's also important because government, financial and health regulations and fines related to data scrutiny have intensified and seriously taken. You should be in a position to answer a variety of questions such as some samples given below and answers to these kinds of questions are central to issues at hand during a typical compliance audit. You need to have systems that monitor and ensure that sufficient data logging and protection is in place.

Oracle EBS auditing and logging functionality give you that capability to answer the following questions:

- Who exactly accessed or changed data within our systems?
- When was that data access or when was it changed?
- How did a specific user gain access to the data?
- Was the change to the database table approved before the change was made?
- Are privileged users abusing their unlimited access?

The most common reasons that administrators are required to configure auditing and logging include the following:

- Monitor for compliance reasons, including SOX, HIPPA, PCI-DSS

- ☐ Perform business process monitoring to implement business controls
- ☐ Monitor performance of the environment
- ☐ Monitor system and database activity
- ☐ Detect suspicious activity and attacks
- ☐ Investigate incidents after an attack

Benefits of an Effective Audit and Logging.

- ☐ Provide accountability of what users are doing
- ☐ Help with compliance requirements
- ☐ Help ensure data integrity and accuracy
- ☐ Allows quality assurance over your change management processes
- ☐ Help you identify abnormal scenarios
- ☐ Used to reconstruct a sequence of events
- ☐ Segregation of Duties
- ☐ Help satisfy both internal and external auditors,Security teams,Technical and Functional system administrators

Good Internal Control

An audit trail allows you to backtrack through a sequence of data events starting from its origination and should as a minimum include the following:

- ☐ Who initiated the event
- ☐ When the event took place
- ☐ The value before the event
- ☐ The value after the event
- ☐ What type of event it was (i.e. the creation of data, the change of data or the removal of data)

Interested Roles or Profiles for this activity

There are a variety of people who may be interested in auditing With respect to different aspects of the Oracle E-Business Suite. Some of them are:

- ☐ External/Internal audit teams and Security teams

☐ Functional system administrators and users

☐ Technical system administrators (Apps DBAs /Core DBAs/ Performance Analysts/ UNIX DBAs)

Conclusion

While the mechanisms described here will be useful for any of the reasons and roles mentioned above, we will be focusing on monitoring the Oracle E-Business

Suite application and technology stack to monitor current usage, how to detect attacks and suspicious activity, and auditing and logging configuration that will allow for a more comprehensive incident investigation after an attack.

Without an audit trail in place,

☐ You are not able to provide this kind of information and can lead to audits taking far longer than expected and you may fail in audit due to having weak internal controls in place.

☐ You have very little visibility of change and so all of the above benefits become problems that you will struggle to overcome.

ORACLE EBS AUDITING AND LOGGING

In this chapter we will see how to configure and use Oracle E-Business Suite audit and logging features with configuration steps and best practices for auditing. It also suggests which common application objects to audit.

To enable AUDITING and LOGGING in Oracle EBS you have to determine what you are going to put into the audit trail (i.e) what "change" are you going to track.

Oracle EBS is a very large and complex suite of applications so the correct approach to building an effective audit trail is to take a targeted approach (i.e)audit only what you actually need.

Understanding exactly what to audit can be quite tricky due to the complexities of the underlying data model in Oracle EBS but this can be greatly simplified by using our own auditing solution and methodology With respect to our business.

What to be Audited (Normally "Non-Transactional data")

Master data

- ☐ Suppliers
- ☐ Customers
- ☐ Products...etc

Key Configurations

- ☐ Profile Options
- ☐ Menus
- ☐ Functions
- ☐ Lookups

Security Setup

- ☐ Users
- ☐ Responsibilities
- ☐ Assignments...etc

Module Setups

- ☐ Purchasing Parameters
- ☐ Payables Parameters
- ☐ Ledgers
- ☐ Journal Sources
- ☐ Approval Limits...etc

High-Risk Functionality

- ☐ Functionality that allows SQL injection
- ☐ Alerts...etc

What Not to be Audited (Normally "Transactional data")

- ☐ Day-to-day transactional data
- ☐ Analytical data
- ☐ Temporary/transient data

☐ Interface data

Sometimes there will be a specific requirement to audit transactional data or unusual data like high-value invoices or payments.

Given below some AUDITING and LOGGING options in Oracle EBS

1. Monitoring of User Activity

This is a very useful screen since it tells you exactly which users are logged in and what are they doing in the system at any point in time. One may check this screen before bouncing or restarting the system to make sure all users are logged out.

The online monitoring of user activity within Oracle Applications is achieved via the Monitor Users form (Form Name: FNDSCMON.fmx).

The navigation path within the Sysadmin responsibility is **Security > User > Monitor**.

In order to activate the capability of this form one has to select an appropriate option for the profile option **"SIGN-ON: AUDIT LEVEL"** Profile Option.

The available options are: -

NONE - No monitoring.

USER - Will only show you a list of logged-in users.

RESPONSIBILITY - Will show you the user logged in and the responsibility they are using.

FORM - Will go down to the lowest level of detail and show you the User, Responsibility and Form being accessed.

Viewing Monitoring Reports about Users and their activity:

Depending on what audit level you have selected for the profile option under discussion you may also generate various reports as indicated below: –

Sign-On Audit Concurrent Requests: View information about who is requesting what concurrent requests and from which responsibilities and forms.

Sign-On Audit Forms: View who is navigating to what form and when they do it.

Sign-On Audit Responsibilities: Used to view who is selecting what responsibility and when they are doing it.

Sign-On Audit Users: Used to view who signs on and for how long.

Sign-On Audit Unsuccessful: Show audit information about unsuccessful logins to Oracle Applications.

2. Unsuccessful Login Attempts

Oracle E-Business Suite automatically stores unsuccessful local logon attempts in

APPLSYS.FND_UNSUCCESSFUL_LOGINS. Only the names of valid users in FND_USERS will be recorded. This functionality cannot be disabled.

Run the "**Sign-on Audit Unsuccessful Logins**" report

Use the **UnsuccessfulLogins.sql** script provided My Oracle Support Knowledge Document 2069190.1

3. Data Changes Tracked with Who Columns

Oracle E-Business Suite tracks data changes automatically within a record in tables. Database rows are updated with the creation and last update information. The system stores this information in the following columns known as "Who Columns":

if you want to see the Who column information of changes to Profile Values for the last ten days, you could use the following SQL:

select p.profile_option_name "Internal name", fpv.PROFILE_OPTION_VALUE value, cr.user_name "Created", to_char(fpv.creation_date,'DD-MON-RRRR HH24:MI:SS') "Creation Date", upd.user_name "Updated", to_char(fpv.last_update_date,'DD-MON-RRRR HH24:MI:SS') "Update Date",to_char(ll.start_time,'DD-MON-RRRR HH:MI:SS') "Login Time" from fnd_profile_options p, fnd_profile_option_values fpv,fnd_user upd, fnd_user cr,fnd_logins ll where p.profile_option_id = fpv.profile_option_id (+) and fpv.last_updated_by=upd.user_id (+) and fpv.created_by=cr.user_id (+) and fpv.last_update_login=ll.login_id (+) and fpv.last_update_date > sysdate-10;

4. Purging Sign-On Audit Data

Purge end-user access data using the Purge Sign-On Audit Data concurrent program.The current program purges all Sign-On Audit information created before a specified date.

The following data is deleted:

- Data for who signs on and for how long
- Data for who is selecting what responsibility and when they do it
- Data for who uses which forms in an application and when

5. Page Access Tracking

Page Access Tracking allows administrators to track application usage statistics and perform Web site traffic analysis. It transparently captures application-rich context information for every user click. In terms of performance, the data capture has negligible overhead. You can do the following.

- Enable and disable Page Access Tracking
- View reports on the gathered data

Examples of Available Reports:

- Page Performance reports per mid-tier node
- Page access flow chart for a given user session
- Search reports based on several filter criteria
- Access reports for a given application, responsibility and/or user across the Oracle Applications Framework, JTF, and Forms tech stacks

6. Debug Logging (Unexpected Logging)

It is often used to diagnosing and debugging problems encountered in Oracle EBS code This log can also assist with diagnosing security problems and detecting security attacks. The default configuration (and the current recommendation) for Debug Logging is set to log information to the database.

The Debug Logging mechanism also supports logging to the file system using the following profile:

AFLOG_FILENAME FND: Debug Log Filename "/path/to/apps.log"

Conclusion

Oracle EBS comes with a lot of AUDITING and LOGGING features.

The important point to keep in mind on AUDITING and LOGGING features is to "only audit and log what you need";

Don't go with "lets audit this just in case" approach'

The key point as to exactly what is needed to satisfy the audit requirements should be analysed and finalised by the business beforehand only.

HOW TO PREPARE THE EBS SECURITY AUDIT REPORT

Summary

The purpose of this exercise is to determine the security vulnerabilities in the Oracle EBS Applications and Oracle Database deployed in the production servers. The internal vulnerability tests should be carried out to identify the vulnerabilities in the internal network which is exposed to a user with malicious intent. The tests should be carried out from the internal network node that has read-only access to the target servers. No penetration test should be out for these systems. You should take due care not to harm the servers or hinder the business functions enabled by these IT systems in production mode.

Approach

- ☐ Information should be gathered on the PROD target systems
- ☐ Security assessment of the database and applications must be done using Scripts
- ☐ Discussion must be made with respective stakeholders to understand existing support process
- ☐ Examination of Existing documents with specific focus to operational policies and procedures should be done
- ☐ Investigate on the Existing Patch, Software Versions and configurations against best practices suggested by oracle and other global security standards

☐ Consolidate the findings and report on the observations, severity, category, Impact and Recommendations

☐ For the security review of the business application and Database, check the management controls such as user wise access controls, customization standards, existing operation procedures for support and day-to-day monitoring, on the third-party system integration/interfaces, operational controls to migrate the development and customization objects, user accounts and password

Scope

SCOPE OF ACTIVITY	DESCRIPTION
Oracle EBS Security and Operations Review	Review of Current Access controls, and ERP Security Administration, operations and management controls of Oracle E-Business application.
Database Vulnerability Assessment	Examine if any potential security threat in the existing configuration of production instance of oracle EBS implemented over the Operating System (O/S) with Oracle Database.

Planned Schedule of the Script Execution

Index	Activity	Start Date	End Date	Time Frame
1	Internal Vulnerability Assessment of Database			
2	Internal Vulnerability Assessment of EBS			

Acknowledgement

As a part of the audit process, the Audit team should interact with several key stakeholders of the business. Audit Team should acknowledge and put on record the valuable inputs provided by the business stakeholders. The name of business stakeholders should be given here.

Summary of Audit Report

Report on Security review of oracle EBS

    1.1.   Report System Assessment EBS Suite:

    1.2.   Report System Assessment – Database:

Key Findings of EBS Vulnerability

EBS			
Vulnerability Category	**Severity Ranking**	**To Be Reviewed**	**As per Recommendation**
Operations	Medium		
	High		
Security	Medium		
	High		
Configurations	Medium		
	High		
DATABASE			
Vulnerability Category	**Severity Ranking**	**To be reviewed**	**As per Recommendation**
Operations	Medium		
	High		

Security	Medium		
	High		
Configurations	Medium		
	High		

Conclusion

The report should end with a conclusion.

Sample EBS Security Audit Report

Executive Summary

This is the report of audit findings and recommendations on the EBS security audit carried over from November 19, 2018 from Nov 23, 2018. The detailed report about each task and our findings are described below. Audit Team ensures that this report context is unbiased and only based on reference to global security standards.

The purpose of this exercise is to determine the security vulnerabilities in the Oracle EBS Applications and Oracle Database deployed in the production servers. The internal vulnerability tests were carried out to identify the vulnerabilities in the internal network which is exposed to a user with malicious intent. The tests are carried out from the internal network node that has read-only access to the target servers. No penetration test was carried out for these systems. Due care is taken not to harm the servers or hinder the business functions enabled by these IT systems in production mode.

Approach

- ☐ Information gathered on the PROD target systems
- ☐ Security assessment of the database and applications using Scripts
- ☐ Discussion with respective stakeholders to understand existing support process
- ☐ Examination of Existing documents with specific focus to operational policies and procedures
- ☐ Investigate on the Existing Patch, Software Versions and configurations against best practices suggested by oracle and other global security standards.

☐ Consolidate the findings and report on the observations, severity, category, Impact and Recommendations.

☐ For the security review of the business application and Database, we checked the management controls such as user wise access controls, customization standards, existing operation procedures for support and day-to-day monitoring, on the third-party system integration/interfaces, operational controls to migrate the development and customization objects, user accounts and password.

Scope

SCOPE OF ACTIVITY	DESCRIPTION
Oracle EBS Security and Operations Review	Review of Current Access controls, and ERP Security Administration, operations and management controls of Oracle E-Business application.
Database Vulnerability Assessment	Examine if any potential security threat in the existing configuration of production instance of oracle EBS 12.2.5 implemented over Solaris SPARC with the database as Oracle 12.1.0.2 Oracle Database.

Summary of Audit Report

Report on Security review of oracle EBS

Report System Assessment EBS Suite:

9 active application users have access to system administrator responsibility.

Application tier components critical patch updates are outdated.

Apps schema username and password are visible in concurrent manager log file.

Role-Based responsibility matrix document is not available.

Report System Assessment – Database:

Several database users have default passwords.

Critical System privileges are available to users with default passwords.

Everyone in the database has access to system data dictionary information.

Non-System users have been assigned with DBA role.

EBS			
Vulnerability Category	**Severity Ranking**	**To be reviewed**	**As per Recommendation**
Operations	Medium	2	
	High	3	
Security	Medium	1	
	High	2	3
Configurations	Medium	3	1
	High	0	

DATABASE			
Vulnerability Category	**Severity Ranking**	**To be reviewed**	**As per Recommendation**
Operations	Medium	1	
	High	1	
Security	Medium	2	
	High	4	
Configurations	Medium	2	2
	High	0	

Key Findings of EBS Vulnerability

1. OBSERVATION: EBS Application tier components latest Security Patch Update (CPU) was not applied on application tier components whereas we observed that Latest PSU (July 2018) was applied on Database oracle home.

Category: Operations

Severity Ranking: HIGH

Impact: Oracle strongly recommends that every Critical Patch Update be applied as soon as possible to minimise the risk of a numerous Database related security attack.

Recommendation: Suggest to apply the latest CPU (i.e., CPUOct2018) in PRODUCTION environment, after proper testing.

2. OBSERVATION: Many Oracle Application users have sensitive page access (Sensitive's marked by Oracle Support).

Category: Operations

Severity Ranking: HIGH

Impact: Application users having Sensitive page access are allowed to view and modify sensitive data from Oracle applications.

Recommendation: Suggested to prepare the responsibility matrix based on the users' role and review whether the users do need all those access.

3. OBSERVATION: Apps username and password are visible in concurrent request log files. Application User who can view this log file can see the apps password and will have full access to the database. This is due to "set –x" environment variable included the concurrent manager script.

Category: Operations

Severity Ranking: HIGH

Impact: Application users will have full access to the database which is a big security concern. Users holding apps schema credentials can maintain, change and modify the data.

Recommendation: Suggest to review the list of concurrent manager files which has "set –x" entry and remove it from the file.

4. OBSERVATION: Purging Sign-on audit data and Purge logs and closed systems have not been scheduled to perform as part of existing Purging routines, the following are the only purging routines, that are executed currently.

USER_CONCURRENT_PROGRAM_NAME	Parameters
Purge Concurrent Request and/or Manager Data	MANAGER, Age, 30, , , , , , , , , Y, Y, , , , , , , , , , , ,
Purge Concurrent Request and/or Manager Data	REQUEST, Age, 30, , , , , , , , , Y, Y
Purge Obsolete Workflow Runtime Data	REQAPPRV, , 0, TEMP, Y, 500, N
Purge Obsolete Workflow Runtime Data	REQAPAME, , 0, TEMP, Y, 500, N
Purge Obsolete Workflow Runtime Data	POAPPRV, , 0, TEMP, Y, 500, N

Purging Sign-on audit data and Purge Logs and Closed System Alerts has not been scheduled to perform.

Category: Operations

Severity Ranking: MEDIUM

Impact: Sign-on audit table and table related to Alerts will grow and will impact the performance of the application usage.

Recommendation: Suggest to schedule the requests to run on a daily basis, there are no suggested parameters for this request, as it depends on the company policy to retain the data.

5. OBSERVATION: Trace has been enabled for the below Concurrent Program.

Program Name	User Program Name	Last Updated By	Description
CCOFSTAT	CCO Program - Customer Statements	X.PLOBOOOO	TD CONSULTANT

Category: Operations

Severity Ranking: Medium

Impact: Trace files will be generated in the database tier for every single run of concurrent request. This will lead to unnecessary and additional disk usage.

Recommendation: Trace needs to be enabled only in NON-PRODUCTION systems, Disable trace for concurrent programs in PRODUCTION systems.

6. OBSERVATION: Public Role has access to UTL_FILE, UTL_TCP, UTL_SMTP,UTL_HTTP,DBMS_LOB packages.

Category: Operations

Severity Ranking: HIGH

Impact:

1. Public roles having access to UTL_File, will allow any database user to access Operating system files.
2. Public roles having access to UTL_TCP, will allow any database user to write and read sockets.
3. Public roles having access to UTL_HTTP, will allow any database user to write content to a web browser.
4. Public roles having access to UTL_SMTP, will allow any database user to send mail from the database server.
5. Public roles having access to DBMS_LOB, will allow any database user to manipulate large objects and BFILE file read access

Recommendation: Revoke the Execute privileges on the following packages UTL_FILE, UTL_TCP, UTL_SMTP, UTL_HTTP, DBMS_LOB from Public role.

7. Below Privileges Directly assigned to the user (name starting with PRR8) and not through Roles (Only Data Access):

GRANTEE	OWNER	TABLE_NAME	GRANTOR	PRIVILEGE	GRANTABLE
PRR8CE	SYS	DBMS_SQL	SYSTEM	EXECUTE	NO
PRR8MRP	SYS	DBMS_SQL	SYSTEM	EXECUTE	NO
PRR8AR	SYS	DBMS_SQL	SYSTEM	EXECUTE	NO
PRR8QA	SYS	DBMS_SQL	SYSTEM	EXECUTE	NO
PRR8OE	SYS	DBMS_SQL	SYSTEM	EXECUTE	NO
PRR8APPS	SYS	DBMS_SQL	SYSTEM	EXECUTE	NO
PRR8RW	SYS	DBMS_SQL	SYSTEM	EXECUTE	NO
PRR8INV	SYS	DBMS_SQL	SYSTEM	EXECUTE	NO
PRR8AP	SYS	DBMS_SQL	SYSTEM	EXECUTE	NO
PRR8PO	SYS	DBMS_SQL	SYSTEM	EXECUTE	NO
PRR8BOM	SYS	DBMS_SQL	SYSTEM	EXECUTE	NO
PRR8GL	SYS	DBMS_SQL	SYSTEM	EXECUTE	NO
PRR8RW	APPS	OE_DEF_CONDN_ELEMS_DFV	APPS	SELECT	NO
PRR8RW	APPS	OTA_COMPETENCE_LANGUAGES_DFV	APPS	SELECT	NO
PRR8RW	APPS	OTA_TRAINING_PLANS_DFV	APPS	SELECT	NO
PRR8RW	APPS	OTA_TRAINING_PLAN_COSTS_DFV	APPS	SELECT	NO

PRR8RW	APPS	OTA_TRAINING_PLAN_MEMBERS_DFV	APPS	SELECT	NO
PRR8RW	APPS	OTA_ACTIVITY_DEFINITIONS_DFV	APPS	SELECT	NO
PRR8RW	APPS	OTA_NOTRNG_HISTORIES_DFV	APPS	SELECT	NO
PRR8RW	APPS	OE_DEF_ATTR_DEF_RULES_DFV	APPS	SELECT	NO
PRR8RW	APPS	OE_ATTACHMENT_RULE_ELEMENT_DFV	APPS	SELECT	NO
PRR8RW	APPS	OE_BLANKET_HEADERS_ALL_DFV	APPS	SELECT	NO

Category: Operations

Severity Ranking: MEDIUM

Impact: Database manageability is at risk, there are Chances of providing wrong or additional access to users, if access provided directly to the users and not through Roles.

Recommendation: Create database roles for the required database access and assign it to users.

8. OBSERVATION: There are 9 active applications users are holding Oracle EBS System administrators privileges.

USER_ID	USER_NAME	RESPONSIBILITY_NAME
9,864	MOBADM	System Administrator
0	SYSADMIN	System Administrator

9,850	SNER	System Administrator
9,938	MWASTART	System Administrator
9,865	MOBDEV	System Administrator
1,379	ATLAS_INTERFACE	System Administrator
8,291	SBORPPS	System Administrator
9,843	MGRYRU	System Administrator
9,848	SMAHAOOIE	System Administrator

Category: Security

Severity Ranking: HIGH

Impact: User holding system administrator responsibility privilege can maintain, change and even modify application data.

Recommendation: Suggest to review whether the users do need system administrator privileges, as per best practices, suggested to create separate responsibility allocating the specific applications functionality.

9. OBSERVATION: Below Oracle EBS Standard Application Users have default passwords.

Apps Users - Default Passwords
GUEST

Category: Security

Severity Ranking: HIGH

Impact: Oracle EBS Standard Applications user have several well-known default username/password combinations. Default passwords may provide unauthorised access to the Applications.

Recommendation: Suggest to change the default application user password or to disable the application accounts.

To change GUEST password – please follow this Support Document: How to Successfully Change the Guest Password in E-Business Suite 11.5.10 and R12 (Doc ID 443353.1)

10. No application user has system administrator privilege and also has a default password. (priority 1)

Category: Security

Severity Ranking: HIGH

Impact: Default password and system administrator privilege will allow for successful application attack

Recommendation: The current setting is as per recommendable standards, since there are no application users having both default password as well as system administrator privilege.

11. Secure APPLSYSPUB Account

Category: Security

Severity Ranking: HIGH

Impact: In EBS APPLSYSPUB is one of the important Account

APPLSYSPUB is a public schema that grants access to the Oracle applications initial sign-on forms. This account is used by Oracle Applications to initially connect to the database and check user password during a user sign-on process before a user is connected.

So we should not revoke or grant unnecessary privileges to APPLSYSPUB account.

Recommendation: APPLSYSPUB account has all necessary privileges and doesn't hold any unnecessary grants, So the current setting is as per recommendable standards.

12. Use Secure Flag on DBC File

Category: Security

Severity Ranking: HIGH

Impact: The Server Security feature of the Application Object Library supports authentication of application server machines and code modules in order to access the database. When the Server Security is activated, application servers are required to supply server IDs (like passwords) and/or code IDs to access a database server.

Recommendation: Since the server security feature is enabled in the application it is as per recommendable standards.

13. OBSERVATION: Retrieve Audit Records Using Standard Reports

Category: Security

Severity Ranking: Medium

Impact: Oracle EBS ships standard reports to access sign-on, unsuccessful sign-on, responsibility usage, form usage and concurrent request usage. The above reports have not been run in EBS environment for the past 50 days.

Recommendation: Suggested to review and use the given standard reports to get details on the above usage

14. OBSERVATION: Database users, listed below, are having default passwords.

USERNAME	ACCOUNT_STATUS
APPLSYSPUB	OPEN
ASN	OPEN
CTXSYS	OPEN
DDR	OPEN
DNA	OPEN
DPP	OPEN
FPA	OPEN
FUN	OPEN

GHG	OPEN
GMO	OPEN
IA	OPEN
IBW	OPEN
INL	OPEN
IPM	OPEN
JMF	OPEN
LNS	OPEN
MGDSYS	OPEN
MTH	OPEN
OSM	OPEN
QPR	OPEN
RRS	OPEN
WH	OPEN
XLE	OPEN
ZX	OPEN

Category: Security

Severity Ranking: HIGH

Impact: Default passwords may provide unauthorised access to the database.

Recommendation: Default accounts should be locked and expired when they are not required for daily operations, and if default accounts are needed, then Passwords of those accounts needs to be changed to a different one (than default passwords).

15. OBSERVATION: Database users who have default password also have critical system privileges

GRANTEE	PRIVILEGE
ASN	Create any outline
	Drop any outline
	Analyse any
	Alter any outline
CTXSYS	Inherit any privileges
DDR	Analyse any
	Create any outline
	Alter any outline
	Drop any outline
DNA	Create any outline
	Analyse any
	Drop any outline
	Alter any outline
DPP	Analyse any
	Create any outline
	Drop any outline
	Alter any outline
FPA	Drop any outline
	Alter any outline
	Analyse any

	Create any outline
FUN	Drop any outline
	Analyse any
	Create any outline
	Alter any outline
GHG	Create any outline
	Drop any outline
	Alter any outline
	Analyse any
GMO	Create any outline
	Analyse any
	Alter any outline
	Drop any outline
IA	Analyse any
	Drop any outline
	Create any outline
	Alter any outline
IBW	Analyse any
	Create any outline
	Drop any outline
	Alter any outline
INL	Drop any outline
	Create any outline

	Analyse any
	Alter any outline
IPM	Create any outline
	Alter any outline
	Drop any outline
	Analyse any
JMF	Analyse any
	Alter any outline
	Create any outline
	Drop any outline
LNS	Alter any outline
	Drop any outline
	Analyse any
	Create any outline
MGDSYS	Inherit any privileges
MTH	Analyse any
	Drop any outline
	Alter any outline
	Create any outline
OSM	Alter any outline
	Create any outline
	Analyse any
	Drop any outline

QPR	Analyse any
	Create any outline
	Alter any outline
	Drop any outline
RRS	Analyse any
	Create any outline
	Drop any outline
	Alter any outline
XLE	Alter any outline
	Analyse any
	Drop any outline
	Create any outline
ZX	Create any outline
	Drop any outline
	Analyse any
	Alter any outline

Category: Security

Severity Ranking: HIGH

Impact: Listed above database users are having a default password and also having critical database privileges, there is a possibility of database security attack.

Recommendation: Suggest to set the complex password to users who have a default password.

16. OBSERVATION : Public Role has system table select access with grantable to yes

Category: Security

Severity Ranking: **HIGH**

Impact: Public role having select access on system tables (Along with grantable to yes), allows any database users to provide access to other database users, which will allow free visibility on critical database information.

Recommendation: Revoke the ability to grant from the public, and also review if the public require select access on system tables

17. OBSERVATION: SPOTLIGHT non-system database user having critical system privileges.

SPOT	SELECT ANY DICTIONARY	YES
	CREATE ANY SYNONYM	YES
	DROP ANY PROCEDURE	YES
	SELECT ANY TABLE	YES
	DROP ANY VIEW	YES
	DROP ANY SYNONYM	YES
	DROP ANY TABLE	YES

Category: Security

Severity Ranking: **HIGH**

Impact: SPOT non-system user will be allowed to perform critical operations like drop and modify database objects of any other database users.

Recommendation: suggest to review the privileges assigned to SPOT database user and revoke them if not necessary.

18. OBSERVATION: Non-system database user has been assigned with DBA role access

Database Users having DBA Access	Account Status
OPS$ORACLE	OPEN
QUEST_SPACEMGR	LOCKED
OEM	LOCKED
VENKATEAAAA	OPEN
BNAAAAAAAAAA	EXPIRED & LOCKED
MAAAAAAAAA	OPEN
DJAAAAAAAAAAA	OPEN
EXPERT	LOCKED
FDAAAAAAAAAA	OPEN
WCAAAAAAAAAA	OPEN
VTAAAAAAAAAA	OPEN
SHAAAAAAAAAA	LOCKED
ASRIAAAAAAAAAA	OPEN
GNAAAAAAAAAAAA	OPEN

Category: Security

Severity Ranking: Medium

Impact: A DBA role is the Critical DB administration privilege through which any database operations can be performed without any control.

Recommendation: Review whether the marked users definitely need DBA Access, else suggested to provide only the required individual database privileges.

19. OBSERVATION: List of non-system database user who has select any table privilege.

GRANTEE	PRIVILEGE	ADM
AKADUUUUUUU	SELECT ANY TABLE	NO
ASRINIVUUUUUU	SELECT ANY TABLE	NO
BLUUUUUUUUUU	SELECT ANY TABLE	NO
BNUUUUUUUUU	SELECT ANY TABLE	NO

Category: Security

Severity Ranking: Medium

Impact: select any table privilege will allow Users to access sensitive data.

Recommendation: Review the list of users who have selected any table privilege. If required, provide select access on specific tables (instead of all tables).

20. OBSERVATION: Debugging Options related to Business functions has been enabled in PRODUCTION servers for few applications users, site and Responsibility level for an extended period of time.

Debug profile options for Multiple Business functions like Project Accounting, Fixed Assets, etc., has been enabled at user, responsibility and Site level

PROFILE_OPTION_ID	APP_SHORT	OPTNAME	D_LEVEL	OPT VAL	UPDATED
11,675	CN	CN: Set Debug Workflow On	SITE	Y	02/04/2015 00:00:00
1,994	FND	Utilities:SQL Trace	USER: MAAAA	Y	02/24/2017 02:55:27
5,540	FRM	FRM: Debug Mode	SITE	Y	08/15/2016 14:44:00
7,473	PO	RCV: Debug Mode	SITE	Y	10/17/2001 00:00:00

Category: Configuration

Severity Ranking: MEDIUM

Impact: It may affect the performance of the applications over a period of time

Recommendation: Debug should not be enabled in PRODUCTION systems, for any testing it is Best Practice to perform debugging in NON-PRODUCTION systems. If for any unavoidable reasons this is done in production then it needs to be reverted at the earliest

21. OBSERVATION: Profile options, having the possibilities of affecting the data integrity by user with malicious intent, has been enabled in PRODUCTION system for an extended period of time.

UTILITIES: DIAGNOSTICS, PERSONALISE SELF-SERVICE DEFN AND FND: DIAGNOSTICS are the profile options allowed for many applications users.

PROFILE_NAME	PROFILE_ LEVEL	LEVEL_VALUE	VAL UE	LAST_UPDA TE_DATE
FND: Diagnostics	User	PNARKHUUUU	Y	03-Apr-18
FND: Diagnostics	User	DDOBUUUUU	Y	24-Jan-18
Attachment File Upload Restriction Default	Site	Site	Y	22-Aug-11
Personalise Self-Service Defn	User	RREIUUUUUU	Y	21-Sep-16
Utilities:Diagnostics	User	SMAUUUUUU	Y	04-Sep-17
Utilities:Diagnostics	User	SBORUUUUU	Y	31-Jul-16

Category: Configuration

Severity Ranking: MEDIUM

Impact:

This Profile option has the possibilities of affecting the data integrity by a user with malicious intent.

- ☐ "Personalise Self-Service Defn" & FND: Diagnostics profile allows the users enabled with this specific profile options to make changes/personalise at the various levels of applications, which cannot be captured through EBS Audit trail.
- ☐ Attachment File Upload Restriction Default: When the profile option "Attachment File Upload Restriction Default" is set to 'Yes', then all files in the fnd_mime_types EBS table for which the flag are set to "Y or default" can be uploaded. This opens a window for Spam files to be uploaded.

Recommendation: Identified application profile options needs to be disabled.

If in case of any specific purpose, then the requirement needs to be addressed through Oracle EBS administrator only.

22. OBSERVATION: Migrate to Password Hash

Category: Configuration

Severity Ranking: Medium

Impact: We can switch EBS to use hashed passwords to better secure the EBS environment. To achieve this you must use the FNDCPASS (or AFPASSWD) command-line utility in MIGRATE mode. (Ref: Note 457166.1).

Note: This process is irreversible.

Recommendation: Hashed Password security is not enabled in the environment. Review the offering from Oracle whether the business needs this.

23. REMOTE_OS_ROLES Database parameter is disabled.

NAME	VALUE
remote_os_roles	FALSE

Category: Configuration

Severity Ranking: Medium

Impact: Setting REMOTE_OS_ROLES to TRUE allows operating system groups to control Oracle roles. The default value of FALSE causes roles to be identified and managed by the database. If REMOTE_OS_ROLE is set to TRUE, a remote user could impersonate another operating system user over a network connection.

Recommendation: Nothing needs to be carried from the business side since the current setting is as per recommendable standards.

24. OBSERVATION Underscore database Parameters has been used

Category: Configuration

Severity Ranking: Medium

Impact: unknown underscore parameters without proper advice from metalink, would impact the database.

Recommendation: Ensure that we have proper advises from Oracle Support on those underscore parameters and if it is suggested removing after any debugging or specific issue, then kindly consider removing those parameters.

25. OBSERVATION: Oracle Database AUDIT_TRAIL Parameter is enabled, but using old auditing method. Oracle has introduced a new feature in auditing called Unified auditing in 12c which addressed some of the current challenges like consolidating all audit trails into a single unified audit trail table and detailed features are given below.

PARAMETER	VALUE
audit_trail	DB

PARAMETER	VALUE
Unified Auditing	FALSE

Category: Configuration

Severity Ranking: Medium

Impact: 12c unified auditing brought some exciting new features.

☐ Grouping audit options into a simple audit policy

☐ Allowing simpler action-based audit configurations

☐ Setting condition-based audit configurations

☐ Exempting users from being audited

☐ Merging all audit trails into a single unified audit trail table

☐ Relying on a read-only audit trail table

☐ Auditing any operation related to audit configuration

☐ Auditing any SYS user auditable action

☐ Separating audit administration duties with audit administration roles, AUDIT_ADMIN and AUDIT_VIEWER

☐ Negligible overhead using System Global Area (SGA) queues for accumulating audit records

Recommendation: Suggest to enable unified auditing.

26. RESOURCE_LIMIT database parameter has been Enabled.

PARAMETER	VALUE
RESOURCE_LIMIT	TRUE

Category: Configuration

Severity Ranking: Medium

Impact: RESOURCE_LIMIT determines whether resource limits are enforced in database profiles. If Oracle resource limits are disabled, any profile limits that are set will be ignored.

Recommendation: Nothing needs to be carried from the business side since the current setting is as per recommendable standards.

ABOUT DOYENSYS

Doyensys, started in December 2006, is a rapidly growing Oracle technology-based solutions company located in the US with offshore delivery centers in India.

We specialize in Oracle e-Business Suite, Oracle Cloud, Oracle APEX Development, Oracle Fusion, Oracle Custom Development, Oracle Database, and Middleware Administration.

We provide business solutions using cutting-edge Oracle technologies to our customers all over the world. Doyensys uses a viable Global Delivery Model in deploying relevant and cost-effective solutions to its clients worldwide. A winning combination of technical excellence, process knowledge, and strong program management capabilities enables Doyensys achieve global competitiveness by making technology relevant to its customers.

We improve business efficiencies through innovative and best-in-class Oracle-based solutions with the help of our highly-equipped technical resources. We are an organization with a difference, which provides innovative solutions in the field of technology with Oracle products. Our clientele across the globe appreciate our laser focus on customer delight, which is our primary success parameter. We have more than 250 resources across the globe. The technical capability of Doyensys stands out from the crowd as we not only provide services of exceptional quality for various Oracle products on time but also take credit for having developed our own products such as DBFullview, EBIZFullview, DBIMPACT, SmartDB, etc.

Our customers are fully satisfied with our services and appreciate our work as we stretch beyond their expectations. We do not compromise on quality for delivery, and the policies of Doyensys revolve around PCITI [Passion, Commitment, Innovation, Teamwork, and Integrity].

Doyensys encourages its employees to participate in Oracle conferences across the globe, and our team has presented papers at various conferences such as AIOUG Sangam, OATUG Collaborate over the years.

The exemplary work of Doyens as a team has created a wonderful environment in the organization. The policies framed by the management are very flexible and employee-friendly, keeping in mind the growth and interest of the organization.

We received 'India's Great Mid-size Workplaces' award (Rank #19) based on the feedback given by our employees in strict confidence and evaluation of various parameters by Great Place to Work. We are an equal opportunity employer and do not discriminate based on sex, religion, gender, nationality, etc. Our women are given a lot of flexibility to work in the organization, understanding the time that they need to spend with their family.

We are also proud to share that we received the award 'Best Workplaces for Women' from Great Place to Work and were ranked among the top 75 in IT and BPM Best Workplaces.

Among the TOP 75 of India's Best Workplaces in IT & IT-BPM 2019

The culture to excel is at the heart of everything Doyens do. We not only share and care for other folks within the organization but also for the folks around the globe.

We have Database and Oracle EBS blogs available on the Doyensys page and are accessible on the internet. These blogs are exemplary work done by Doyens from the knowledge and experience gained by supporting various customers across the globe. There is a habit of creating reusable components for the teams within Doyensys so that a similar piece of work can be helpful for some other project within the organization.

The management is very supportive and encouraging, which is very much visible from the awards [Passion and Commitment, Commitment and Customer Delight, Rookie of the Year] that are given to Doyens, who excel in various categories.

Doyensys is not only a great place to work but is also a great place to learn as employees are always encouraged to explore new technologies and suggest innovative ideas that can benefit the clients. The teams within Doyensys are always encouraged and recognized by the management to add value to the work that is delivered to the customer rather than just doing monotonous work.

ABOUT THE AUTHOR

ASIF HUSSAIN

 Asif Hussain, an Oracle Database professional with 14+ years of experience, specializes in Oracle e-Business Suite Database Administration and other Oracle products with rich exposure to support Fortune 500 clients in the USA, India, Middle East, and other countries. He is a cloud evangelist specializing in Oracle Cloud Infrastructure and also has expertise in supporting other databases such as MS SQLServer. He is an author, blogger and distinguished speaker at Oracle conferences across the globe including AIOUG Sangam (2017, 2018, and 2019) and OATUG Collaborate (2018). He holds a Bachelor's degree in Engineering from the University of Madras and a Masters in Business Administration in the field of Information Systems. He is certified in ITIL, COBIT, and is also an Oracle Certified Professional (OCP) for Oracle Database 9i,10g,12c, Oracle Cloud, and is an Oracle Certified Expert (OCE) for Oracle RAC 11g. He weaves the best solutions with his rich expertise in Oracle cloud to ensure the best enterprise architectures for customers. He is currently a Project Lead for DBA Practice with Doyensys. Asif is an amateur tennis player and enjoys playing the game during his pastime.

GOBINATH RADHAKRISHNAN

Gobinath Radhakrishnan works as a Senior Principal Consultant at Doyensys and is a Computer Engineer. He has 10 years of Oracle experience working with major clients. He has rich experience in Oracle Database and applications. He was awarded the 'Best Employee of the Year' for educating employees and customers about the Linux platform. His completed certifications include Oracle Database Administrator (12C) and Oracle Cloud (OCP). He is interested in investments in stock markets and enjoys cooking on holidays. He loves to play cricket and is also an ardent fan of integrated organic farming.

PUSHPARAJ VIJAYAN

Pushparaj Vijayan is an Oracle Certified Professional 11g and 12c, Oracle e-Business Suite R12 Applications Database Administrator Certified Professional. He focuses mainly on Oracle Database High Availability, RAC Cluster, Data Guard, Backup and Recovery, various methods of upgrade and database migrations. He has rich experience in various projects of Oracle Application and Oracle Administration, extensively working on Oracle Database and Application. At present, he is working as a Senior Principal Consultant in Oracle Database and Application Administrator in Doyensys. He was recognized several times by the organization for 'Delighting the Customer' in 2015, and for 'Passion and Commitment' in 2017. He is fascinated by meditation and yoga.

NIRMAL KUMAR VEERARAGHAVAN

Nirmal Kumar Veeraraghavan is a Project Lead at Doyen System with 15 years of exclusive experience in Oracle EBS Applications and Core Database, which includes administration, installation, migration, upgradation, support and he also has functional knowledge of Oracle SCM modules. He also worked as a freelancer in the field of EBS Administration. He holds a Master's degree in Computer Application and is an Oracle Certified Database Administrator and Oracle Application Server Administrator. He is interested in learning new things, especially emerging cloud technologies. He is a divisional football player and enjoys cooking with his family during his free time.